AF423377

Vanquish and Triumph in Jesus Christ

Paul Talafo

Vanquish and Triumph in Jesus Christ

Job Daniel Jean

Other books from Paul Talafo :

- Le disciple que Jésus-Christ cherche - *Au bon souvenir de Marie Madeleine*
- Les premiers seront les derniers et les derniers seront les premiers - *Qui sont-ils ?*
- Du sacerdoce lévitique au sacerdoce du Christ, la lumière sur le salut par la grâce au moyen de la foi - *Sur le fondement des apôtres et des prophètes*
- Un cœur brisé et contrit ou la repentance, la gratitude et la couronne des vainqueurs
- Les écluses des cieux aux héritiers de Dieu et cohéritiers avec Christ sur la terre en ce temps-ci
- Naître par l'Esprit, Vivre par l'Esprit, Marcher par l'Esprit, Prier par l'Esprit, Libérer par l'Esprit

Unless otherwise indicated, all Scripture quotations are from the electronic Modern King James Version (eMKJV).

VANQUISH AND TRIUMPH IN JESUS CHRIST

Paul Talafo, 2018

ISBN: 979-10-94949-10-8
Printed in the United States of America
Copyright © 2018 by Paul Talafo

Job Daniel Jean
Ministère chrétien pour l'enseignement
job.daniel.jean@gmail.com

This book is an English translation of the French book *Vaincre et triompher en Christ Jésus*

Copyright © of the original French book 2017
By Job Daniel Jean

Table of Contents

Introduction

In keeping with the promises of Jesus Christ, Christians are waiting for His imminent return. What attitude should Christians have in this waiting since the resurrection and departure of Christ to heaven where He sits now at the right of the Father?

This question is fundamental because it addresses the quality of Christians' life on earth today. It is constant, according to the words of Jesus, that Christians are no longer of this world because their city is upcoming, heavenly: The Heavenly Jerusalem. These are the words of Christ as confirmed by the Apostles.

Not being of this world, which life do Christians have to deal with? The following words from the Bible give us an overview:

> **«*To him who overcomes* *I will give to eat of the tree of life, which is in the midst of the paradise of God»*** **(Revelation 2:7).**

«***He who overcomes*** *will not be hurt by the second death*» (**Revelation 2:11**).

«***To him who overcomes*** *I will give to eat of the hidden manna, and will give to him a white stone, and in the stone a new name written, which no man knows except he who receives it*» (**Revelation 2:17**).

«***He who overcomes*** *and keeps My works to the end, to him I will give power over the nations*» (**Revelation 2:26**).

«***The one who overcomes****, this one will be clothed in white clothing. And I will not blot out his name out of the book of life, but I will confess his name before My Father and before His angels*» (**Revelation 3:5**).

«***Him who overcomes*** *I will make him a pillar in the temple of My God, and he will go out no more. and I will write upon him the name of My God, and the name of the city of My God, the new Jerusalem, which comes down out of*

> *heaven from My God, and My new name»* (**Revelation 3:12**).

> «***To him who overcomes*** *I will grant to sit with Me in My throne, even as I also overcame and have sat down with My Father in His throne»* (**Revelation 3:21**).

These words of Christ are addressed to the winners. These are the Christians the Lord Jesus Christ expects at His upcoming. How would it be otherwise since, according to the Scriptures, Jesus Christ is the Lion of Judah? Can Christians hope to become less than their Master this Lion? Absurd isn't it?

As we go through the book of Revelation, we would be tempted to say that these events relate to a distant future, that of the upcoming of Jesus Christ, and not to the present. Such thinking is not meaningless. However a Bible scene reveals Jesus' anger towards the disciples who had failed to deliver a demoniac. Jesus then shouted at them:

> «*O faithless and perverse generation, how long shall I be with you? How long shall I suffer you? Bring him here to Me»* (**Matthew 17:17**).

If in addition, the fact that nothing resisted Jesus during His earthly journey – He interrupted the storm, changed the water into wine, multiplied the bread, walked on the water, raised the dead, healed the blind, the deaf, the dumb, the paralytic and the demonic –, we harm no one in recognizing that Jesus Christ, the Lord of glory, was a winner. Not only did He triumph over His death on the cross the third day, but since the start of His earthly pilgrimage three years earlier, He had been triumphing over any obstacle standing His way.

The above Bible verses define Christian morality when facing the challenges of this world: **Christians must overcome and triumph over all obstacles standing their ways, as their Lord did during His earthly journey**. For God wants and longs for His children to triumph on the earth, at this time and in the future, at the expected return of Jesus Christ.

The purpose of this book is to expose the posture of Christians triumphing during their earthly life, now and until the return of the Lord Jesus Christ. They will know how to stand the right posture when facing the challenges of the earth, so many challenges.

This book has nothing to do with programs of eminent gurus on *the art of war*. There are also programs on market-winning strategies. None of these strategies were used by the victors of the Bible: Abraham, Isaac, Jacob, Joseph, Moses, David, Daniel, Mordecai, Esther, Apostles. The peculiarity of these heroes is that it is by God only, with God and for God that they triumphed. The present book will therefore expose the necessity of triumphing with Christ and only Him, without the wisdom of language, but only with the power of His Word.

The words 'Christian', 'Disciple', 'Saint or Holy' will be considered perfectly equal, as well as 'Bible' and 'Scripture'.

Unless otherwise notice, all Bible quotations are from the Modern King James Version (MKJV). They are pasted in this book for a reason. **Matthew 5:10-13** means *the book of Matthew, chapter 5, verses 10 to 13*. For the sake of truth, we were careful to mention each Bible verse with respect to the historical context, highlighting the essential part in **bold**. The reader may find boring the full reproduction of Bible verses rather than footnotes. This was done on purpose because memorized verses tend to suffer discrepancies as time passes. Is it due to memory failure or evil action? We presume a bit of both. Is this why the Israelites, after a long period of obedience, began to transgress the commandments of God? Possible. We note that Moses instructed the Israelites to *bind the commandments for a sign upon their hand, as frontlets between their eyes, and to write them upon the posts of their house, and on their gates* (**Deuteronomy 6:8-9**). This warning of Moses is not fortuitous. The reader is therefore invited not to be exasperated with the reproduction of the Scriptures, but rather to read them studiously. He will notice that some verses which he thought he had memorized well, come in a different way. We have put in boxes very important notices. Finally, all the pronouns referring to the Lord God have been put in capital letter, for the sake of both accuracy and God's holiness. May the Lord God accompany you reader, open your mind and intelligence to seize the length and depth of His love for the men and women He approves of, in addition to His call to the first resurrection. Indeed "*Blessed and holy is he who has part in the **first resurrection**. The second death has no authority over these, but they will be priests of God and of Christ, and will reign with Him a thousand years*" (**Revelation 20:6**).

The triumph of the heroes of faith

The triumph of Abraham

The patriarch Abraham, accompanied by his wife Sara and nephew Lot, left Our-of-Chaldeans for an unknown destination, moved only by the call of God. Only once in Canaan did Abraham receive a visit from the Lord God, who told him that his descendants would inherit the land Canaan he had just trodden – Israel today.

The scriptures show that his wanderings on the Promised Land were not without danger. First, his wife Sara was barren, which exposed him to leave this world heirless. Second, he armed three hundred and eighteen soldiers to free his nephew Lot made prisoner in a local conflict.

It was not all done. A severe famine forced him out from Canaan to Egypt where the Pharaoh took away his wife Sara, presented then by Abraham as his sister to save his life. Another famine produced the same effects later on, on the eve of his hundred years, in the kingdom of Gerar. Each time,

God came to rescue the couple who escaped with great goods.

After several years of waiting, Sara, then aged ninety, gave birth to her son Isaac. The hundred-year-old patriarch could then fire for business forever, ready to enjoy a happy old age. But unfortunately, God asked him to offer his son Isaac in sacrifice. Abraham complied. However during the process, God stopped the patriarch before his hand reached the young man deadly. A lamb was offered as a replacement.

After Sarah's death, one of Abraham's servants led a mission to find Isaac's future wife. The mission miraculously succeeded and Rebecca, a distant relative of Abraham, became Isaac's wife. The couple welcomed twins Esau and Jacob (Israel).

The Scripture records the end of the patriarch's life in these terms: "*These are the days of the years of Abraham's life, which he lived: a hundred seventy-five years. And Abraham expired and **died in a good old age, old and satisfied**. And he was gathered to his people*" (**Genesis 25:7-8**).

This verse concludes, without any doubt, that Abraham triumphed over all the trials paving his road at his time. It must be made clear that without trials none can speak of triumph.

The triumph of Joseph

Joseph, son of Jacob and grandson of Isaac, was the firstborn of Rachel the favorite among the four wives of Jacob. After many peregrinations, Joseph received the birthright on his father's twelve sons, while he only came in eleventh; the eldest son Ruben having been deposed for dissolute conduct. It was Jacob's special affection for Joseph that drove his jealous brothers to set a plot against him. They sold Joseph to a slave trader who sold him to a high Egyptian priest (**Genesis 37: 2-28, 36**). Joseph found himself in Egypt against his will, at a tender age, far from his father and his younger brother Benjamin, son of his mother Rachel. From a pampered son, he became a slave in Egypt, without right or freedom. He suffered not to see his parents for more than twenty years, until the mighty hand of God made him governor of Egypt. A position he took advantage of to reconnect with his parents, and make them immigrate to Egypt land, in the midst of a world food shortage (**Genesis 39:1 to 46: 6**). Joseph could have died sooner after the sexual assault he was unjustly accused of by the high priest's wife. What slave would survive such an accusation coming from the mistress of the house, at a distant time when masters had the right of life and death over their slaves? The high priest rather sent Joseph safe to prison.

Joseph's stay in prison was not without danger. If even today prisoners die in their cells because of difficult living conditions, what about three thousand five hundred years ago when barbarism and savagery were widespread?

In becoming the governor of Egypt, after all these tribulations, Joseph triumphed royally and died at the end of a happy old age, surrounded by his brothers, repentant criminals.

The triumph of David

David, still a celebrity today as his victory over Goliath has been recalled over centuries, was the youngest of an Israelite family of the tribe of Judah, comprising seven boys. While his older brothers were fighting the Philistines somewhere at the battlefield, David was watching over his father's sheep. His daily life was then made of sheep to feed and milking, in addition to various cares. The profession of shepherd was common in Israel because of millennial tradition. The Israelites were shepherds of small cattle, from father to son.

It was then that one of the most famous stories of humanity occurred: *David versus Goliath*. The history reveals that the Israelites had camped for several months against the

Philistines, the latter proposing, to close the war, a duel between their champion Goliath, an imposing colossus, and a valiant soldier to chose in the Israelites army. Goliath was so imposing that the Israelites were afraid to meet the challenge, and the situation had been going on for months. It was a chance visit to his older brothers that David heard Goliath's blasphemous remarks to a timid army of Israel. The end-of-story is known: David challenged Goliath and killed him. This day was a great victory for Israel.

David was elevated to the rank of national hero and army general. He could then go out and claim many military victories for Israel. Later, he ascended the throne of Israel, not without having escaped several plots set by his predecessor. David was able to triumph over all the trials on his way to kingship and during his reign. More importantly, Goliath's weapons adorned King David's armory throughout his life.

The triumph of Job

Job was a rich and famous Israelite, the *greatest of all men of the East* according to the eponymous book of the Bible. He was blessed materially, spiritually, and feared God. He was not like those wealthy people whose riches distort the sense of wisdom. In addition to be the father of seven boys and three daughters, Job owned the most important herds of the kingdom of Israel, all cattle and goats combined. In his desire to prove that Job's faith relied most on material blessings than godliness, Satan asked for permission to test him.

In a succession of misfortunes, Job lost in one day all his ten children and goods. The devil also smote him with leprosy to test him more (**Job 1:1-2; 2:7**). From the high social status he once held, Job fell apart and became the laughing stock of everyone. Despite his misfortunes, Job refrained from cursing God as the devil hoped. Having successfully passed this terrible test, God restored Job. He regained his former glory. God gave him again seven boys and three girls considered the most beautiful girls in the kingdom. Job welcomed his sons and grandsons until the fourth generation. He recovered twice his former possessions (**Job 42:10-17**). Once the most respected man in the East, Job fell apart, became very poor, before being rehabilitated after the difficult ordeal he passed through successfully. This is the triumph of Job in the midst of his tribulations.

The triumph of Ruth of Moab

Ruth, from the eponymous book of the Bible, was from Moab, wife of an Israelite living in the land of Moab. Unfortunately for Ruth, her husband died heirless. Her brother-in-law followed the same path. Made unhappy by this terrible fate, her mother-in-law Naomi, a widow of the tribe of Judah, dismissed her stepdaughters in order to come back alone to Israel, her homeland. Ruth refused to separate from her mother-in-law despite Naomi warning on an uncertain future in a country she did not know.

So Naomi landed in Israel, accompanied by a young widow of a foreign origin, Ruth of Moab. At the time of the Old Testament, the widow was in the same social class as the orphan and the immigrant in Israel. Ruth's social status was aggravated by the fact that she was a foreigner, a status the Israelites truly abhorred since marry a foreigner meant to unite with foreign gods, an abomination condemned by the Law of Moses.

Thanks to her mother-in-law's advice, Ruth tied herself to a wealthy relative, Booz who, according to the Law of Moses, had the right of redemption to perpetuate the name of the parent deceased heirless. Booz was aware of the young woman's misfortunes, as well as her attachment to the homeland of Israel, of which she knew very little. Booz ended up marrying Ruth. From the lineage thus created, will be born David, ancestor of Christ (**Matthew 1:5**). From a low status of a foreign widow, Ruth became a historical figure in the lineage of David and Jesus, a true triumph over the trials of life.

The triumph of Mordecai and Esther

Esther, from the eponymous book of the Bible, was an Israelite deported to a foreign land, a Jewish slave of sorts. Following the advice of Mordecai her relative, also deported and on duty at the royal palace, she entered a miss beauty contest to choose the queen of a kingdom covering hundred and twenty-seven provinces. This kingdom was so great at time that the contest could be compared to the Miss Universe contest today.

Esther won the contest and became queen, wife of the king. She was able, with the help of Mordecai, to counter a plot to exterminate all Jews of the kingdom. The Jewish people worldwide recall this historic event every year during the Purim Festival. While Esther and Mordecai – newly appointed prime minister – were promoted to the first places of the kingdom, Haman the Amalekite, former prime minister and author of the anti-Jewish plot, was hanged at the pylon previously prepared by him for Mordecai.

From the low status of deportees and all the inconveniences related to it, Esther and Mordecai triumphed and became queen and prime minister of the greatest kingdom of the world.

The triumph of Daniel

Daniel of the eponymous book of the Bible, was deported at the same time as the royal court, during the first campaign of Nebuchadnezzar, king of Babylon, against the kingdom of Judah. Daniel was part of the royal family, a well-educated class. Despite this privileged status, Daniel was a slave, far from his native Jerusalem where he could come and go, worship at the temple as he pleased. Indeed Daniel was pious. His stay in Babylon-land did not go without danger. Upset by a dream, the king of Babylon threatened to kill all the astrologers and sages who would not give him the meaning of the terrific dream he had just had. The king refusing to give them any detail of the nightmare made the situation worse. The king asked that astrologers revealed both the content and the meaning of the dream. He feared that by giving them a tip, these scholars would draw a logical picture for the sole purpose of escaping death. The king especially thought that the dream had a divine origin; he wanted to know more about God's plans for the kingdom today and in the future.

Seeing the sword come closer, considered one of the wise scholars of Babylon, Daniel promised the king an answer. His request was granted and the persecution suspended. By this promise, Daniel took a major risk because, in case of failure, he was in the front line to be beheaded.

Thanks to God, the content and the meaning of the dream were revealed to Daniel. The king was so impressed that he gave him superiority over all the scholars of the kingdom, as well as appointing him governor of the district of Babylon. His triumph was unparalleled at the time.

The triumph of Apostle Paul

Paul (Saul of Tarsus) was a Law doctor in Israel, of the tribe of Benjamin, circumcised on the eighth day, Pharisee and disciple of Gamaliel, chief rabbi in Israel. Paul had the profile of an accomplished man. He must naturally have been a source of pride for his family and the religious party he belonged to. He was by far an estimated person for the Jewish Council of Jerusalem, who gave him right to bind and drag for judgement any Jew convicted of following Jesus Christ. This mission was accomplished with great zeal to the point of perpetrating the death of deacon Stephen, a treasured Christian of the first century (**Acts 7:58**).

On his way road to Damascus, encouraged by his successes against Christians, he met Jesus Christ in a terrific scene. The Lord then turned him into a powerful tool for propagating the gospel he had been fighting (**Acts 9:1-20**).

Considered a traitor by the party of the Pharisees he once served, Paul was persecuted in Jerusalem and abroad. The

Jews did not stop tracking him wherever his name was invoked in his apostolic missions. It is no surprising that he was falsely accused of all kinds of crimes. To escape his opponents, Paul had to hide and be rescued by Christians of his time. One of these plots took him chained before Emperor Caesar in Rome. By demanding the justice of Caesar, rather than the biased one from the Jews of Jerusalem, Paul long delayed the outcome of his trial to testify Christ before the powerful, the governors and a crowd of peoples. Peter paid him a vibrant tribute (**2 Peter 3:15**). Paul spent the last fifteen years of his life jailed, defending the gospel of Jesus Christ.

Paul is today, two thousand years later, the most prolific and widely read Bible writer, having signed and co-authored more than half of the New Testament books. In his days he worked more than all the disciples of the first hour, those who had accompanied Jesus in His earthly ministry. He refused all material advantages of his time by zeal for the Lord.

The triumph of Mary Madeleine

Mary Madeleine, whose history has been surprising in the Christian world for centuries, was a sinner converted to Christ. True versions of the Bible portray her as a prostitute. Her sister was Martha and her brother Lazarus. This family lived in the city of Bethany in Israel, a family that Jesus loved so much. Lazarus was also resurrected by the Lord Jesus Christ four days after his burial. As is still the case today, the social class of the prostitute was of the lowest in Israel. Mary Madeleine was therefore, at best, a woman of very low social status.

However, thanks to repentance and forgiveness of sins, she became a servant of the Lord Jesus Christ, a vessel of noble use, useful and proper to every good work (**2Timothy 2:20-21**). She received a very rare tribute from the Lord because Jesus was not easily impressed: *Truly I say to you, wherever this gospel shall be proclaimed in all the world, this also that she has done will be spoken of for a memorial of her* (**Mark 14:9**). According to the Gospel of John, she is the first person Jesus revealed Himself to after rising from death (**John 20:15-17**). These are distinctive signs of a person Jesus cherished a lot. Mary Madeleine, originally a prostitute, came out victorious in the history of salvation.

The triumph of Jesus and His Apostles

Born on the earth with a low social status – born in a nauseating manger – Jesus carried out His huge and heavy mission on earth. Let's save what everyone knows and point out that Jesus and His Apostles are the most read authors in the world, year in and year out. No famous author or publisher has been up to challenge Jesus and His apostles.

Triumph: The only way out of the Lion's life

> «*For so has Jehovah spoken to me: as the lion roars, even the young lion on his prey when a multitude of shepherds are gathered against him, **he will not be afraid of their voice, nor fret himself because of their noise**. So Jehovah of hosts shall come down to fight for mount Zion, and on its hill*» **(Isaiah 31:4)**

> «***Behold, the Lion of the tribe of Judah, the Root of David**, has prevailed to open the book and to loose the seven seals of it*» **(Revelation 5:5)**

By constantly reading the same Bible verses, we have become accustomed, by omission, amnesia or fashion effect, to overlook the way they relate to our lives in real. Thus, despite the recurrent use of the term Lion to refer to Jesus Christ in the Bible, very few people make the connection between the Lord and this scary beast. It took the Holy Spirit to draw my attention to this word for a long time, so that I can imagine its effects on Christians' lives. What does that imply? To say that Jesus is the Lion of Judah is not new, since we hold this truth of the Bible. It is rather the continuation that intrigues. *What is the lion's kid?* The Holy Spirit asked me. *It is a lion's descendant Lord* was my answer. *Does the lion's kid have the spirit of his father lion? Yes Lord! Without a doubt*, I replied. *Do you think that the disciples of Jesus, who received the Holy Spirit – the Spirit of Jesus – have the Spirit of a Lion?* I was dumbfounded by this turn of phrase, a brainstorming exercise that unfortunately Christians are not used to when it comes to the Bible. Clearly, I immediately understood that the disciples of Jesus Christ – the Lion of Judah – are also lions. How can one have the spirit of a lion without being a lion? This truth has very rarely touched the minds of nowadays Christians. Before his victory over Goliath, had King David not used to tear the bear when he was energized by the Spirit of the Lord (**1 Samuel 17:34-36**)? The disciples of Jesus Christ (Christians) must be aware that they are lions. A lion is not afraid. The lion's spirit is not a spirit of timidity. The Spirit of Christ, which the Christian has received, is not a Spirit of timidity, but *a power and of love and of a sound mind* (**2 Timothy 1:7**).

What do we know about the lion-animal in general? He is not afraid of anyone. He is the scariest animal, considered the king of the jungle where he lives. As soon as he leaves his lair, he has a sure step, the serenity of a king who dreads nothing. Other animals are afraid of him and tremble at his roar. He is at the top of the food chain. In the verse **Isaiah 31:4** recalled above, it is with a reason that the Lord compares His doing to that of the lion: *As the **lion** roars, even the **young lion** on his prey when a multitude of shepherds are gathered against him, **he will not be afraid of their voice, nor fret himself because of their noise**. So Jehovah of hosts shall come down to fight for mount Zion, and on its hill.* Here God makes no difference between the lion and the cub. It's the same seed.

Should the Christian live in fear (who is endowed with the Lion Spirit, a powerful Lion because it relates to Jesus Christ)? Why should the Christian live in shyness, and be afraid to reveal himself as if his enemy, Satan, held a sword of Damocles on his head?

The truth is that the Christian is a lion like his Master Jesus Christ. As much as Christ was never afraid during His earthly pilgrimage, so much the Christian, His disciple, has no reason to be afraid. Rather he must be the most relaxed person in the world, as calm as a lion in his lair.

The reason why the Lord asks His disciples to turn their cheeks, to make an extra mile, or to give up a second tunic, has nothing to do with weakness. Rather, it is because the Lord believes that His disciples are strong enough to bear these inconveniences. Do they not possess the Holy Spirit, the Spirit of truth, the Comforter? They are lions. Thanks to the Spirit of truth they possess, Christians are more armed than people of the world. The Christian therefore has a strong endurance ability that allows him to carry his cross as the Lord has recommended to him (**Luke 14:27**).

The Christian triumphs over the bonds of blood

The influence of blood's bonds on humans cannot be underestimated. Men are sensitive to the bonds of blood: father, mother, uncle, aunty, brother, sister, cousin, nephew, close and extended family, etc. These links deeply matter on humans. Even the heroes of the Bible have not escaped the strength of these ties.

Abraham fought victoriously over the kings who had taken his nephew Lot prisoner (**Genesis 14: 14-16**). In the eyes of Abraham, his nephew was very important to the point of going to rescue him with three hundred and eighteen warriors.

After Joseph had revealed to his brothers that he was the famous governor of Egypt, he gave Benjamin, his junior brother (son of his mother), five times the portion given to his half-brothers (**Genesis 43:34**). In his eyes, Benjamin mattered much more than his half-brothers. The latter were sons of his father, but not those of his mother.

Because his two eldest sons were burned by the foreign fire brought on the altar against the Lord's command, the high priest Aaron could not eat the part of the holy meat that the investiture procedure imposed on him (**Leviticus 10:1-20**). It was because he had just lost his two eldest sons.

Apostles Paul and Barnabas had a hot dispute and parted ways because of John Mark, whom Paul blamed for showing little interest in the Lord's work (**Acts 15:37-40**). Barnabas kept John Mark with him because they were cousins (**Colossians 4:10**). We can see how the blood ties have affected the mission of the Lord, even in the days of Apostles.

The truth is that blood ties have nothing to do with the way of salvation; and that the Christian would do well to be wary, as Jesus Christ was wary of His family ties including Mary, His mother.

Please beware! This is not to say that blood ties do not interest the Lord. This is not the meaning of this chapter. Remember just that blood ties should not thwart the Lord's work. For the Lord Himself, during His earthly mission, made no concession either to His mother Mary or to His biological brothers: James, Joseph, Simon and Jude (**Matthew 13:55**).

Jesus always took care to keep His mother away from the mission His Father had entrusted to Him. Jesus was not commissioned WITH His mother and biological brothers. He was the ONLY missioned for the salvation of humanity. The separation of Abraham and Lot, the nephew he cherished so much, gives us a glimpse of this principle of separation between the flesh and the work of God. It was once after the two parted ways that God revealed to Abraham the mission that was his: to become the ancestor of Christians. Lot and his descendants, despite the blood ties with Abraham, had nothing to do with the divine mission entrusted to his uncle Abraham. This can be difficult to admit in humans accustomed to recognize full of virtue in blood. But it's God's decision, and God knows why He separates the flesh and the Spirit.

The confusion about *"Who God has He missioned?"* has often been the source of quarrels among the biological brothers of a servant of God, some believing to be entitled to the sacred mission on the sole basis of blood ties. Let us remember the incident which broke out in the desert between Moses, Aaron and Miriam, biological brothers and sister, on the question of who was the prophet the Lord had missioned. Aaron and Myriam publicly contested to Moses, their junior brother, the exclusivity of this role (**Numbers 12:1-15**). Although Aaron assumed a major role in the Levitical priesthood and the temple of God, God left no doubt as to who was His messiah in freeing Israelites from the Egyptian servitude. His servant Moses was the only messiah. Aaron and Myriam were collaborators only.

So Jesus Christ firmly insisted that there be no doubt about the salvation of humanity. He is the only Savior of humanity, His mother and biological brothers having nothing to do with it. Jesus' biological brothers, James and Jude, played a role in the church after the resurrection and departure of Jesus Christ to heaven, because they believed in the Lord and not because of blood ties. During the lifetime of Jesus on earth, Mary and her other sons did not hold any mandate in the mission of salvation.

To convince ourselves of this, let's look at the following writings:

> *«Then one said to Jesus, behold, **Your mother and Your brothers** stand outside, desiring to speak with You. And He answered and said to him who told Him, **who is My mother? And who are My brothers?** And He stretched out his hand toward His disciples and said, behold, My mother and My brothers! For **whoever shall do the will of My Father in heaven, the same is My brother and sister and mother»*** **(Matthew 12:47-50)**.

In these verses, Jesus clearly pointed out His primacy in the mission of salvation, at the same time as He denied to His biological family any role in this mission. Jesus further states the following:

> «*If anyone comes to Me and **does not hate his father and mother and wife and children and brothers and sisters, yes, and his own life also**, he cannot be My disciple*» (**Luke 14:26**).

With these words, there is no doubt that Jesus already foresaw a standoff between Christians and their biological parents regarding faith in Christ. More importantly, Jesus explicitly stated that the Christian could be forced to break his blood ties in order to make his faith alive. Of course, the Bible verses above are not an appeal to family conflict between the Christian and his loved ones. Jesus says that if parting ways is the only condition for salvation, then the Christian must move on despite the family drama.

By saying, **whoever shall do the will of My Father in heaven, the same is My brother and sister and mother** (**Matthew 12:50**), Jesus draws a red line between the Christian Church and blood ties. For the Christian henceforth, his true brothers, sisters, mother and father are the ONES who do the will of God, his heavenly Father. Apart from this short-list, the Christian must not recognize the title of spiritual parent, even if he is dealing with biological family members. His parent is only one who does the will of his heavenly Father. It may seem cruel. But is there anything more cruel than the death of Jesus on the cross? If God has gone so far as to give His only Son as sacrifice, is it so hard for the Christian to respect this separating line? Believe me, these biological parents will not die. They will be shocked, nothing else. But Jesus died for the Christian. Jesus did not ask any Christian to die on a cross similar to that of Golgotha. He only asks that the separating line be respected on the question of the new kinship of the Christian, for the sake of the latter.

The heirs of God are victors

> «*And if we are children, then we are heirs;* **heirs of God and joint-heirs with Christ***; so that if we suffer with Him, we may also be glorified together*» **Romans 8:17**.

Christians must question themselves about why the Bible is written in the language of men and not that of angels. The obvious answer is this: not being an angel, no man would read a Bible written in angels' language. The other answer that seems to elude many is that God wants us first to interpret His word with human intelligence. Unfortunately for many, words do not seem to have the same meaning when they relate to God. Why? Because, for no apparent reason, men have decided so no matter the will of God. God does not agree because He once blamed the Israelites for honoring Him only with lips **(Isaiah 29:13)**. Note that there is a scene in the Bible where God explicitly blamed the Israelites for showing more respect for men's tradition than His Word **(Jeremiah 35:14)**.

I always wondered why such a terrific reality. Not that I have the answer, but this thinking has been enabling me to always read the Word of God. The comments I am going to give you result from that investigation: *What would happen if I am to become heir of the richest man of the world?* Men would unroll the red carpet under my feet. *True* was the answer of the Holy Spirit. *What if I am introduced, not as heir of the richest man of the world, but rather that of the Almighty God?* I think Lord that the whole planet would more than unroll the red carpet under my feet. The Holy Spirit then said: *Yet this is how I see the Christian!* According to **Romans 8:17** indeed, the Christian is *heir of God and joint-heir with Christ.*

Even if the whole world does not give Christians so much importance, the Holy Spirit's reproach to Christians is that they don't take themselves seriously as they should do. The world will not respect a Christian who does not take himself seriously. Let us remember the attitude of the Jew Mordechai to the Amalekite Haman – **Book of Esther**. Mordecai never bowed before Haman the Amalekite, although the latter was the prime minister of the kingdom. This posture of Mordechai could be explained by the fact that God had commanded Jews to put an end to Amalekites' being under heaven (**Exodus 17:14, 16 and Deuteronomy 25:19**). Although the Jews did not take this command seriously at time, Mordecai took care of it.

Christians must regularly question the posture they should have, and remember that they are heirs of His heavenly Majesty, joint-heirs with Christ.

Can the heir of God lose? No way! The children of God triumph in all circumstances, whether favorable or not. The difficulties faced by Christians are always occasionally and not perennial. The Christian must always triumph over his foes.

The Christian being the heir of God – a victor thus – he must adopt during his new life a conqueror's posture. To win is one thing, but victory can succeed defeat and vice versa. So we can have a succession of failures and victories. This is not what is discussed in this chapter. The conqueror's posture is rather that of the one who triumphs ALWAYS. It is the status of the Christian: a perpetual an eternal victor. The Christian always triumphs. That's why the victor's posture must stick to his skin.

David's posture against Goliath

The Bible's record referring to King David perfectly illustrates the victor's posture the Christian must show.

> *«David spoke to the men who stood by him (...)* **Who is this uncircumcised Philistine that he should defy the armies of the living God?**» (**1 Samuel 17:26**)

> *«David said to Saul, let no man's heart fail because of this Philistine.* **Your servant will go and fight with him**» (**1 Samuel 17:32**)

> **«Your servant killed both the lion and the bear.** *And this uncircumcised Philistine shall be like one of them,* **since he has defied the armies of the living God**» (**1 Samuel 17:36**)

The Bible text above relates to David speaking to King Saul of Israel, before battling Goliath. We can take note here of David's posture during the talk. David was never shaken by Goliath appearance nor by the terror inspired by him whereas the whole army of Israel was petrified (**1 Samuel 17:11**). David dwelt on the Word of God, the fundamental truth, like this: ***Who is this uncircumcised Philistine that he should defy the armies of the living God?*** For David, it was unthinkable for a human to challenge the troops of God. Why? Because first, God is almighty. It is therefore risky to challenge Him. Secondly this challenge was initiated by an uncircumcised. No matter how majestic he may look like, an uncircumcised was firstly an uncircumcised to the Israelites, the people of Covenants.

For David, his upcoming victory over the giant Goliath was not questionable. We can see it from the conversation he had with the colossus just before the fight:

> *«You come to me with a sword and with a spear and with a javelin. But **I come to you in the name of Jehovah of hosts, the God of the armies of Israel, whom you have defied. Jehovah will deliver you into my hand today, and I will strike you and take your head from you and give the bodies of the army of the Philistines to the birds of the air today, and to the wild beasts of the earth, so that all the earth may know that there is a God in Israel»*** (**1 Samuel 17:45-46**).

The whole story is known.

David's assurance is surprising here. How could he know without a shadow of a doubt that *he will strike the Philistine and take his head from him*? This is the winner's posture. The winner does not doubt because he knows the result in advance. He is a winner for a reason. Jesus defeated the world and the enemy on the Golgotha Cross. The Lord demands Christians to accept that they are victors thanks to Jesus' victory over the world and Satan at Golgotha: "*Now shall the prince of this world (Satan) be cast out*" (**John 12:31**); Jesus said to them: *In the world you shall have tribulation, but be of good cheer. **I have overcome the world** (**John 16:33**).

By saying: *I have overcome the world*, Jesus told the Christian that no matter the tribulations he will be going through in the world, he can be sure that he will come out victorious because He, the Lord, has already triumphed over the world.

The fear of nowadays Christians is similar to the fear of the people of Israel during the Goliath's challenge. Scripture records that *Saul and all Israel heard those words of the Philistine, and they were dismayed and greatly afraid* (**1 Samuel 17:11**). Then came David who put the dots on the 'I'. The Christian must always remember that he is the son of God, heir to the King of kings, joint-heir with Christ now and forever. **It is not at the return of Christ that the Christian will claim his position as heir of God. He is already that**

heir! When Christ returns, the Christian will receive his inheritance. At that time, he will no longer be heir but owner. For now, he must keep the profile of worthy heir of his heavenly Father and not tremble. That pagans not roll out the red carpet before him is not essential. What matters is that the Christian keeps in mind that he is the child of God, cherished by his Father. And he will see the glory of God as David in the above narration.

David's posture during the wars of Israel

Another Bible scene describes the posture of the Christian facing enemies.

> «*You have also given me the neck of my enemies; so that I might destroy those who hate me. (...) Then **I beat them small as the dust before the wind; I cast them out like the dirt in the streets**. (...) **A people whom I have not known shall serve me. As soon as they hear of me, they shall obey me; the sons of strangers shall bow down to me. The sons of strangers shall fade away and be afraid out of their strongholds**»* (**Psalms 18:40-45**).

These Bible's verses relate a scene in which David triumphs over his enemies in a battle. David was a warrior, known to have never lost a battle during his lifetime. He describes the attitude of the defeated in front of him: They are ***afraid out of their strongholds***. There is no doubt that the shadow of defeat had never crossed the mind of this great warrior. He even rejected this option out of the three punishments God proposed in retaliation for one of his blunders (**2 Samuel 24:13-14**).

To a certain extent, the Christian lives in a battlefield where the devil and his armies are constantly attacking him. Jesus recommends to the Christian to *watch and pray*. Such is the posture of the winner. He never asks a question, he wins because he is victorious to the glory of Father God.

Triumph over the fear of dying

Will the Christian escape physical death? This is not what this chapter claims. We say rather that death must stop being taboo among Christians. Unfortunately, this subject makes Christians as cautious as those in the world. What is the use of being a Christian if the question of death continues to maintain psychosis and superstition as with those of the world?

Jesus yet uninhibited the question of death in His Christians as the following words:

> **«God is not the God of the dead, but the God of the living»** (Mark 12:26-27).

Faced with the distress of Christians of his time, Apostle Paul was already calling out of the terror of death with these words:

> *«I would not have you ignorant, brothers, concerning those who are asleep (dead),* **that you be not grieved, even as others (pagans) who have no**

> ***hope****. For if we believe that Jesus died and rose again, even so God will also bring with Him all those who have fallen (asleep in Jesus)»* (**1 Thessalonians 4:13-14**).

These words, like many others in the Bible, tend to mitigate the terror of death among Christians. In fact, according to the Bible, Christians should no longer be terrorized by death, unlike pagans who make all kinds of phobias on the issue.

Apostle Paul added:

> *«For we say this to you by the word of the Lord, that we who are alive and remain until the coming of the Lord shall not go before those who are asleep (dead). For the Lord Himself shall descend from heaven with a shout, with the voice of the archangel and with the trumpet of God. And **the dead in Christ shall rise first**. Then we who are alive and remain shall be caught up together with them in the clouds, to meet the Lord in the air. And so we shall ever be with the Lord. **Therefore comfort one another with these words**»* (**1 Thessalonians 4:15-18**).

The fear of dying is paganism. It is of the world. Not that death isn't sad. It will always be. But for Christians, this dark perspective should not scare as to the people of the world. Because the after-death is extraordinarily more pleasing for Christians. Apostle Paul claimed in his time that he preferred death to life because by his death he would go to meet God, which was far better for him. However, because of the work that awaited him in favor of the Christians, he agreed to remain among them. This is what he said in these terms:

> «*For to me **to live is Christ, and to die is gain**. But if I live in the flesh, this is the fruit of my labor. Yet I do not know what I shall choose. For I am pressed together by the two: having a desire to depart and to be with Christ, **which is far better**. But to remain in the flesh is more needful for you. And having this confidence, I know that I shall remain and continue with you all, for your advancement and joy of faith*» **(Philippians 1:21-25)**.

The Christian knows that death will happen one day or another. Same goes for the pagan. However, when the Christian is pleased with this perspective, the pagan is rather so frightened that he is unable to speak freely about it, unlike Apostle Paul and the Christians.

Triumph over ignorance by reading and practicing the Bible

If there is a statement regularly made in the Church, it is the lack of interest in reading the Bible among many Christians. Several reasons are mentioned. We often hear arguments about the size of the Bible or lack of interest in reading in general. Sometimes we mention memory failure.

Without questioning the above arguments, let's start by pointing out that a weak reading of the Bible helps to put, between God and us, a thick wall that will go more and more thicken. Note also that an emotional father is eager to talk to his children. Just as earthly fathers and mothers love to talk to their children, so does Father God enjoy talking to His Christians. Can we imagine a child not doing everything to know his parents? Absurd isn't it? It is this absurdity that characterizes Christians today. Their reluctance to read the Scriptures does not plead their cause before God.

Christians are often afraid, like those in the world who do not know God. This fear usually lies in ignorance. The more we know, the less we are afraid. Education has in most countries pushed back the frontiers of ignorance, a source of superstition. Not that superstition has disappeared, but regular scientific discoveries tend to mitigate its importance.

The more Christians read the Bible, the more the light of God penetrates and settles in their minds for their happiness. How will God converse with His children if they do not read the Bible? God loves secret interchange with His children (**Matthew 6:6**). These conversations revolve around the Bible, which has more than one hundred and fifty thousand verses. Several times, I have attended speaking-in-tongues relating specific episodes of the Bible. Those aware of these stories knew what they referred to, while others had to inquire, without guarantee of success. For the word of God is meditated regularly under the watchful eye of the Holy Spirit. When a revelation rises from a Bible verse, the one who reads the Bible on a regular basis does not take long to grasp the meaning of it, unlike the one who rarely reads the Bible.

By filling his life with Bible verses, the Christian offers God many opportunities to evaluate his understanding of the Scriptures. The purpose of God is to root the Christian in His holiness so that the latter does not get moved by all kinds of doctrines, but has a true image of Him.

Being the sword of the Spirit, the word of God is a powerful energizer of the Christian life

«*Take the helmet of salvation, and **the sword of the Spirit, which is the word of God**» **Ephesians 6:17**.

«*And these words which I command you this day **shall be in your heart**. And you shall carefully teach them to your sons, and shall talk of them when you sit in your house and when you walk by the way, and when you lie down, and when you rise up. **And you shall bind them for a sign upon your hand, and they shall be as frontlets between your eyes. And you shall write them upon the posts of your house, and on your gates**» **Deuteronomy 6:6-9**.

The Holy Spirit will not be effective in the life of a Christian who does not devour the Scriptures. It's like a car without fuel. The car will not move. It's like a tuneless phone set. It won't ring. Two key words deserve our attention: (i) the soul of man has a penchant for rebellion. That is to say, without a binding discipline, a Christian should not expect his soul to encourage him to read the Scriptures; (ii) without knowledge of Scriptures, the Holy Spirit will lack fuel to function properly in the Christian. A Christian can perfectly feel the inner touch of the Spirit – ointment – but without the help of Scriptures, it will be hard to stick an understanding to that feeling.

As recalled in **Deuteronomy 6:6-9** above, the Christian is invited to devour the Scriptures, to fill his life with them. Thus the Holy Spirit will always put a word of knowledge and wisdom in the mind of the Christian, on every occasion favorable or not. The prophet had promised that God would inscribe His Law on the hearts and no longer on the stone tablets of Mount Sinai. It is the Holy Spirit, present in the spirit of the Christian, who represents this Law. Scripture explicitly states that the Spirit of the Lord is also a Law: *The law of the Spirit of life* in Jesus-Christ (**Romans 8:2**). It is this Law that will react in the life circumstances of the Christian. Provided that the Christian binds his life on the Holy Scriptures.

It will happen very often that the Christian feels an inner touch – ointment – without being able to stick a meaning to this touch. It is little by little that the Spirit will fix the Christian's intelligence on specific Scriptures recorded in his memory. But if the Christian does not know these Scriptures, he will stick only to the perceived touch, nothing more, which could be disabling. This Christian sees but can not explain. He does not help many others.

Let's suppose the Lord does not approve a preaching. The irritation will evidently grow in the Christian's spirit – seat of the Holy Spirit. But without knowledge of Scriptures, he will not be able to disassemble the preacher's errors. Let us remember the temptation of Jesus by the devil. The devil quoted Scripture verses to manipulate the Lord. But the Lord also invoked Scriptures to counter the devil. It is not enough to be irritated in one's mind because of a pernicious preaching, it must be dismantled point by point to be relieved. The drama is that the sermons are always recorded in the memory of the listener. These sermons return in a loop in the memory of the Christian. If these sermons are of the Lord, the Christian will take benefit. Otherwise, he will be confused. But how will the Christian dismount a pernicious preaching if he knows very little about Scriptures? As Jesus did against the tempter, only memorized scriptures will constitute a solid bulwark against such manipulations.

Forcing our soul to read the Scriptures

Let us not forget that it is in our human spirit – not in the soul – that the Holy Spirit sits at the instant you become a Christian. The soul of the Christian is not the seat of the Holy Spirit. Like intelligence and will, the soul is subject to change. King David already summoned his soul to praise the Lord. Here are some excerpts regarding this illustrious hero:

> *«My soul shall make its boast in Jehovah»* (**Psalms 34:2**).

> «*Why are you cast down, O **my soul**, and moan within me? **Hope in God**; for I shall praise Him for the salvation of His face*» (**Psalms 42:5**).

> «***Wake up, my soul**! Wake up, harp and lyre! I will awake the dawn*» (**Psalms 57:8**).

> «***My soul, be silent only to God**; for my hope is from Him*» (**Psalms 62:5**).

> «***Bless Jehovah, O my soul**, and forget not all His benefits*» (**Psalms 103:2**).

> «*Praise Jehovah. **Praise Jehovah, O my soul**» (**Psalms 146:1**).

By these words, the Christian is invited not to yield to laziness or to the rebelliousness of the soul. For example, our body particularly enjoys staying in bed in the morning, warm under a thick blanket. The Christian must then summon his soul to stand up and thank God before starting the day.

Many Christians think that by submitting to the soul, they will perceive the Holy Spirit's will, which they assimilate to those moments when the soul aspires to meet God. It happens to the soul to feel the desire for spirituality, despite its general tendency to rebellion. But if the Christian sticks to this free will, he will see his spiritual life going down.

How to read the Bible? The best way to read the Scriptures, despite their thick volume, is just to read them. It is recommended to follow a discipline according to each one disposition. On a personal basis, we recommend that every day a Christian reads one or two chapters, taking care to mark the end of the last chapter to avoid re-reading and omissions. Once started, a chapter must absolutely be finished because the beginning of a chapter recalls the context of the narration to grasp all the nuances. It is not recommended to stop at mid-chapter. In this case, next time you will have to restart the whole chapter. I usually read until the page is turned – for a paperback Bible. This is my discipline: the end of the chapter, after turning the page, is a good indicator to pause. So next day, my reading will begin at the page marker. Thanks to this discipline, I hardly make mistake on the chapters already read and those to be read; and the whole Bible is devoured in two years. Then a new cycle starts again. This is also the reason why we suggest to read the Bible from Genesis to Revelation, in that order. If a Christian reads everyday chapters on a random basis, he will not be able to maintain a rigorous discipline, let alone telling in which level of reading he is – start, middle or end of Bible. The above strategy needs to be adjusted in case of an electronic Bible.

The wrong method is to devour many chapters in a row, especially during holidays, as it will be difficult to replicate this performance on a consistent basis. Then one will state that the Bible is a hard-to-read book. Then one will postpone the next reading. But reading small quantities according to the above planning, guarantees the Christian continual spiritual nourishment to the satisfaction of the Lord. He will then see his reading become more effective, he will have permanent talks with the Lord, kind of rich supper.

Swallow the daily milk of the Word of God. We insist that it is necessary to read the Scriptures bit by bit as the daily milk before starting the day. We recommend that there is no interruption of more than one day. Usually, at the end of a book, I give myself one day break before moving to the next book – 66 books in a common Bible. We recommend that you do not allow more than one day off unless special circumstances. The problem is that it is difficult to re-motivate one soul after a long pause, because bad habits take over. Two or three days break are not fatal, but bad habits having hard skin, it is better to shorten the pause so that it does not extend indefinitely. It is also a bad idea to delay Scripture reading until summer vacation. It's like depriving a baby of his daily milk, thinking that he will have plenty of time on the weekend. The growth of the baby will be slowed down. As will be slowed the progress of the Christian who does not maintain a constant discipline in Bible reading.

Protect his reading from devil's disturbances. The moment of reading the Scriptures is dreaded and disturbed by the devil. So we advise Christians to protect their readings to avoid the many disturbances of which the enemy has the secret: drowsiness, fatigue, sudden priorities, etc. The enemy knows how to provoke seemingly legitimate needs when the

Lord's moment arrives: the crying baby, a telephone call, an urgent need in and out. Protection is done by asking the Lord to cover with the blood of Jesus the time and place chosen to read and pray, to ward off all the attacks of the devil during reading and praying. May the Lord protect your thoughts against negative and positive distractions. If the enemy knows how to hide behind legitimate needs, God is above circumstances legitimate or not. The most favorable time for reading is around six in the morning at waking. This moment can be slightly delayed on weekends and days off.

Usefulness of other Christian books. What about other books published by Christians? Can one maintain a reading of Scriptures alongside reading other religious books? The works of the saints contribute to the spiritual nourishment of the Christian, since these works regularly rely on Scriptures. These works therefore maintain the spiritual milk the Christian needs daily. However, if in parallel with the reading of other religious books, the Christian maintains a lite reading of Scriptures such as, for example, a chapter every two days, instead of a chapter every day, then it will be perfect, one does not exclude the other.

God takes pleasure when His child goes in His Word. God is always delighted when His children discover the Scriptures to stick on. God will therefore bring complete joy to those who make it their habit and put His Word in practice as explained below. So it is noticed that whoever likes reading will read more; not only the Bible, but also other books inspired by God. While one who does not read the scriptures will increasingly have hard time reading them. This is the lesson taught by the Lord: *To him who possesses, it will be added to infinity; but to him who misses it, even the little he possesses will be taken away.* We must therefore take good habits and not let anything go. The more you love the Scriptures, the more God will reveal to you the nuances and diamonds that are hidden there. The process is long but profitable in terms of spiritual and material blessings. It's about creating your own addiction to the Word. Such an addiction is more auspicious than other addictions of life.

Living proof. My personal case can serve as an illustration of the above. You will see for yourself, through this book and many others in my collection, how much I am immersed in the Scriptures. When the Holy Spirit makes a chapter necessary, Bible verses flow as I pass on the message of the Lord. As soon as a verse comes to mind, I take care to check the source so as not to miss anything, using the most popular versions of the Bible. Why? Because they are buried in me for more than thirty years of meeting with the Lord of glory. Some will argue that the human brain is very skilled. One thing is certain, to date, science has not been able to establish any limit to the human brain. However, if it was about brain genius, I would have never believed. Just figure out that when a Bible verse always arrives at the right time – among hundred-and-fifty-thousand verses – to face a threat or confirm a truth, that it is always the day a collaborator defaulted, that suddenly it comes to you to read more deeply his report and to detect the blunder, and this happens hundreds of times, it is difficult for you to put these coincidences on the stroke of luck, unless chance is as powerful as God. No, it is the work of the Holy Spirit among Christians following the path Jesus Christ set in His time. The desire to read the Bible is probably due to the fact that I am at beginning a scientist, and for the sake of scientist way, we like to check more by ourselves than to copy from third parties, even though these are useful to the body of Christ. We do not need to be scientist to have this approach. The fear of being insidiously manipulated by the most educated was also my motivation. By drowning in Scripture at the beginning of my faith, I was able to wrap myself with the Word as a filter for all the words and advices I received, regardless of personality: brother and sister in Christ, pastor, veteran, deacon, prophet, spiritual guide, elder, etc. I used to relaunch an interlocutor by mentioning very precisely a verse related to the topic of discussion, to make sure nothing was misunderstood from a verse, and to know the feeling of my interlocutor on such command of the Lord. Believe me, by this discipline, I was able to find my way out of many difficult situations, along with refreshing the memory of many. This discipline has also been used in my relations with the non-Christian world, especially the business world. This is to avoid sinning or irritating God like those Christians who are faithful on Sundays but faithless the other days where they behave like pagans. If you find it difficult to read one or two chapters a day, read in just the bearable amount such as one or two paragraphs, while making sure to indicate the end of reading for a quick recovery that will save you boring repetitions. And the Bible will be completely devoured too.

The Lord has not indicated a volume of daily reading. This is just a proposal from an experienced person with no desire to impose anything. But the Lord exhorts to watch and pray, which necessarily comprises the reading of His Word. Come on dear reader! You will get there like that illiterate widow whose story is related below.

Do you know an ancient book that we continue to devour with appetite two thousand years after its publication? The Bible is that book. This indicates that the Bible is the book of the immutable truth of God. Old books have been abandoned because their contents have not passed the trial over centuries; scientific discoveries making these books obsolete. The Christian can therefore trust the revelations of the Bible.

He who does not devour the Holy Scriptures is like an employee who ignores the rights and obligations he is bind to. He is likely to be told by the judge that he has crossed the line, that he does not meet the conditions for the claimed compensation.

He who does not devour the Holy Scriptures is also like an heir who does not know the heritage he is entitled to, a legacy defined in the testament which he does not want to read.

He who does not devour the Holy Scriptures is still like one who lets himself be struck and stepped on. He takes blows that he should not. He does not know whether he should be hit or not, where the blows should come from, whether the blows he should land are allowed or not.

He who devours the Holy Scriptures is rather a wise man who knows, understands and anticipates everything to the glory of God the Father.

Story of an illiterate widow who read the Bible

Fifteen years ago, I visited an old woman in her sixties, whom I knew to have not gone beyond class one of elementary education. The story is that her late husband, himself low educated, ended the learning program his wife was following because one day she got mark A at a test. The man was afraid that his wife would embrace an exciting career at the expense of him, a rather modest husband.

As a widow, she really was illiterate. She could mumble as possible familiar language coming from radio and hearsay.

What caught my attention during my visit was the big Bible opened on her table, a Bible taken from her late husband's affairs. Knowing she was illiterate, I showed her my surprise. She understood and informed me that she was reading the Bible well. I exclaimed then: How do you, who have not passed class one of elementary school? Her answer was that she had always been curious to know what the old Bible found in her husband's affairs could contain, a husband she had never seen reading the Bible, as far as she could remember. She confessed that when her husband forbade her to pursue the teaching course recalled above, she had already learned the basics of ABC. Thus, by combining this technique with radio listening and hearsay, she was able to identify the words of the Bible and their meaning.

I was amazed by what I was watching: an elderly woman, illiterate, widow, who from rudimentary materials, had managed to forge her way to the Word of God, the sword of the Spirit. Hallelujah!

With that, I realized that at the end of time, this widow will rise up to judge those who had several excuses not to read the Scriptures. What could be the strength behind this desire to discover the Holy Scriptures? Determination. She wanted to know what God said to the men and women of this world. And she succeeded.

There is therefore no excuse for those who do not read the Scriptures.

Always practice the word of God to better understand it

Jesus said to His disciples:

> «*Therefore whoever hears these sayings of Mine, and does them, I will liken him to **a wise man who built his house on a rock***» **Matthew 7:24**.

> «*If you know these things, blessed are you **if you do them***» **John 13:17**.

Whoever lingers long in front of a mirror is at risk of trivializing the scar found on his face. It is the mirror effect, the self-manipulation: we think we are pretty and see only the good side of things, not the scar though present. A scar that, alas, people outside will notice first. It is to avoid self-abuse from reading the Bible that the Lord enjoins His Christians to put His word into practice, and not to simply read it.

By dint of reading the Bible and only the Bible, without putting it into practice, we are only reading one of those fiction stories the world is full of; stories that enter left side and leave right side, without leaving a significant trace, if not confusion in a well stuffed memory.

To understand the Word of God, you have to be practical. From the moment we believed, it is better to keep a simple lifestyle that comes down to looking, hearing and acting according to Scriptures.

Do you want to reply to a verbal or physical attack? Answer according to Scriptures, imitate Christ and His Apostles. Are you angry with your neighbor? Follow the Bible that commands to *let anger pass away*. Does someone want to borrow from you? Do not turn away from the borrower. Are you mistaken in a milieu? Greet the people there as much as possible – provided the greeting does not payback bitterness against you.

Have you been criticized like being too fat (girls most often) or that you'll never succeed? Put everything in the hands of the Lord God who alone knows all things, what happens and when it happens. Our body was given to us by the Lord long before the foundation of the world. God defends the work of His hands and is not ashamed of it. You are pretty and you will succeed. Don't be distracted by noises skillfully distilled by the devil.

Were you denied the promotion that you deserved, for the benefit of someone less qualified than you? The devil is accustomed to get you out of your hinges. Do not be alarmed because *it is a grace, if for conscience toward God anyone endures grief, suffering wrongfully* (**1 Peter 2:19**). Rejoice because your enemies confirm that they are not of light.

Do you interact with a brother, a sister or the pastor of a church? Be vigilant and stay on your guard. Answer according to Scriptures. On this, concerning the management of church affairs, it is not recommended to establish the government hierarchy of the world in the Church of Jesus Christ. To manage the world, there is an executive hierarchy accepted and desired by God. However, the Lord refuses that this hierarchical mode settles in His church where He is the only true Head, and not the pastor who claim the role at his expense and misfortune. In his day, James rebuked those who treated Christians according to social status (**James 2:9**). We also know that Paul was not kind to Apostle Peter, convinced of hypocrisy (**Galatians 2:11**). If Paul had taken into consideration the government hierarchy of the world, he would have ignored Peter's hypocrisy, Peter being ten years older than Paul in Christianity.

Do you go through an existential crisis? Glory to God! The Holy Spirit will reveal to you a corresponding scene in the Bible, so that you identify with the Bible hero who triumphed over it.

By pursuing this discipline relentlessly – by definition the disciple follows a discipline – the Christian will realize how accessible and easy to read the Bible is. It's a living story.

Do you fear being insulted, treated wrongfully? Are you afraid that your physique gets despised? Are you worried about being underestimated and overlooked? Are you afraid of gossip, slanders and other malicious remarks? You will be surprised by this answer: All this will happen to you because Jesus Himself and His disciples faced it, and warned that it would happen to Christians at all times, from yesterday to today. Jesus says indeed:

> *«Blessed are you when men **shall revile** you and **persecute** you, and **shall say all kinds of evil against you falsely**, for My sake»* (**Matthew 5:11**).

Apostle Peter added:

> *«For **this is a grace**, if for conscience toward God **anyone endures grief, suffering wrongfully**. For what glory is*

> *it if you patiently endure while sinning and being buffeted?* ***But if you suffer while doing good, and patiently endure, this is a grace from God.*** *For you were not called to this? For* ***Christ also suffered on our behalf, leaving us an example, that you should follow His steps***» (**1 Peter 2:19-21**).

There is no need to panic when this happens. What is important, however, is why will these things happen to you? First, because Jesus warned that these things will happen to His beloved Christians. And there is a reason to it: the devil. The latter always encouraged exploiting the appearance thoroughly, because it is his appearance and splendor that pushed him to rebel against the Almighty God. He knows something about it and has made it his business. By recommending us a position of humility, Jesus helps cut ties with the devil, removes the major asset Satan relies on to divide and reign. Satan is therefore helpless when a Christian suffers without fighting back. Satan loses his most formidable weapons against this Christian. This is why Jesus says, *"Retribution is mine!"* That is to say: *"Cool down dear disciple! Hand everything to Me. I am in control now."*

The most difficult thing – especially at the beginning – is to bear the inconvenience without reacting because, from the world we came from, we used to fight back. But it is here that faith comes into action. Faith says to believe what is unseen. Which means that the Christian, so attacked, must agree to do nothing because the Lord claims the right to reply in his place. All those who have had this experience know, and the Bible confirms it, that God is not used to rushing promptly against the wicked. This is disgusting for the human mentality accustomed to fightback without delay because otherwise, the wait is painful. Imagine the boy who unjustly slaps his comrade. If the latter cannot reply the slap right after, he cries because he hardly supports the injustice done to him. Inaction in the face of injustice can also cause the villain to conclude that you are weak, and encourage him to repeat injustice indefinitely. But the Lord knows that and means His words. He demands to trust Him. Having been there many times, I can personally confirm that IT WORKS! Provided you trust the Word of the Lord.

It is by recapping the misfortunes of the wicked, over time, that we discover how true the Word of God is. The time taken by the Lord to respond is justified by the fact that God is patient with the man He cherishes to the point that He has given His only-begotten Son as sacrifice for salvation. By dint of patience, the Lord ends up raging against the unrepentant and recidivist sinner. The Bible says that *the Lord raises the righteous who falls seven times. But where the wicked stood, there is nothing left.* The villain is therefore overthrown once and for over. The patience of the Lord is justified because the wicked comes to judgment once. He is struck once, without recourse, when it is given to the Christian to fall seven or more times, and the Lord will always raise him up. This is to be understood by the words of Christ inviting to forgive not only seven times, but until *seventy times seven* (**Matthew 18:21-22**).

It is therefore in practicing that we will understand the Word of God, will be encouraged to read it in depth. *Whoever looks into the perfect law of liberty and continues in it, **he is not a forgetful hearer, but a doer of the work**. This one shall be blessed in his doing.* (**James 1:25**).

The Christian triumphs over all crises

«*For a just one falls seven times, and rises up again*; *but the wicked shall fall into evil*» (**Proverbs 24:16**).

It is almost impossible for a Christian to avoid going through one or more crises in his life. Abraham went through several crises, two of which are summarized below. First, when his wife Sara was taken by the Pharaoh of Egypt, a country where famine had forced the couple to surrender; secondly, when on the point of conceiving the promised son – Isaac – another famine forced him to go to the kingdom of Gerar where the same misadventure awaited him. Isaac also – son of Abraham – and his wife Rebecca went through the same drama as Abraham in the kingdom of Gerar. Joseph, son of Jacob, was sold as a slave by his brothers against his will. Because of a persistent famine, Jacob and his seventy members family had to immigrate to Egypt. We know the hardship experienced by Daniel when, deported far from his native Jerusalem, he became an eunuch at the palace of the king of Babylon where many trappers were waiting for him. Job went through one of the worse dramas a man has ever faced on earth – see his Bible eponymous book.

The Christian must prepare to face all the crises he will be going through his lifetime. Just as the heroes of the Bible have triumphed over their misfortunes and their enemies, the Christian has the guarantee that he will have victory at the end of the trial.

No matter the origin of the crisis, of the sin or of the yoke, the Christian must not panic like those of the world. Every crisis experienced by the Christian generates a bunch of teachings under the control of the Lord. Although we do not wish anyone to go through drama, we must recognize that it produces more results than just reading the Bible. Generally, when the crisis occurs, the Holy Spirit – the Comforter – revives in the memory of the Christian, the corresponding case described in the Bible. The Christian will personally make comparisons to understand what is going on. The Christian will soon note that some Bible hero went through the same experience. This search for correspondence will encourage the Christian to read the Bible deeply and relentlessly, at least the part related to his situation.

Many crises affect Christians. Without being exhaustive, we may mention: mourning and tragedy, physical and verbal aggression, job loss, marital separation and divorce, illness, disappointment and frustration, exclusion, homeless, exile or forced immigration. The Christian must be assured that the Lord will help him overcome all these crises, with the added bonus of being able to explore the Bible in depth. The

Christian should not panic above all – easier to recommend than to experience, we truly admit it – but we maintain that the Christian should not panic every time a crisis occurs. He will even be surprised at the calm that is his in a storm. It is the Holy Spirit who is at work at this time. The Christian must be aware that the Lord will accompany him throughout the drama. The Lord is methodical and faithful. He will successfully rescue the Christian and draw praise from the mouth of the latter.

The Bible: the only rule of the Christian life

Someone might also say that the Bible is the contract between a Testator (God) and His joint-heirs (Christians). This may surprise at first. How can the Bible govern the life of the Christian in a law-regulated city like the one we live in? This is a main concern.

The answer comes from Jesus who, by saying *Let the dead bury their dead*, implied that the national laws were intended for the dead – pagans. Then what! Is Jesus wrong when He says pagans are dead? Do Scriptures not indicate that Christians are alive and pagans dead? No offense! Christians are alive and pagans dead. Jesus is not ashamed of His words, even if they are hard at times. Do the abominations and the continual decadence of the earth not suggest such words? Are we at the end of our surprises on the propensity of this earth to generate abomination in defiance of the Word of God who created it?

He who is sincere will recognize that, dealing with the requirements of God's holiness transcribed in the Scriptures, the laws of the earth are rather lax. He who honors the law of

God will be far above the morals of this world, so perfect is the law of God. When Jesus was on earth, He was simply blameless. It was by Jealousy that Pharisees and priests found default in Him by asserting, for example, that He was doing His miracles for Satan's sake. Many peoples, even soldiers of the occupying Roman army, came to beg Jesus for miracles. Every Christian who regularly observes the command of God will see that no law of the earth can resist him when it comes to morality. In fact the Christian's life will be so holy that pagans will have to choose between begging him to reveal the God he serves or hating him out of sheer jealousy – the second option is usually chosen in this decadent world.

Does that not make the Christian a handsome man? Absolutely. The Christian is handsome because he keeps the command of God. Pagans are ugly because first they are dead, second they do not keep the command of God, and they are even incapable of it because it is by the help of the Holy Spirit – whom pagans do not have – that Christians obey God.

The Christian with all parts of his life is therefore invited to comply with the Holy Scriptures without fail. Then he will see the glory of God on a regular basis. His house will be really built on a rock: *The rain came down, and the floods came, and the winds blew and beat on that house. And it did not fall, for it was founded on a rock.* (**Matthew 7:25**).

The Christian triumphs over suffering by suffering

«He suffering in the flesh has been made to rest from sin» **1 Peter 4:1**.

Like every human being, the Christian dislikes to suffer. We can understand it. Throughout the Bible, we discover the suffering of the heroes of faith. None of them escaped it. From Abraham to Apostle John, through Moses, Job and Jesus Christ, suffering spared no one.

The common denominator to all the sufferings of the heroes of faith is that all have triumphed over their trials. Despite his tribulations, namely those misfortunes that occasionally deprived him of his wife Sara, Abraham died of a happy and fulfilled old age. At the end of his earthly journey quite eventful, Moses blessed the children of Israel, tribe by tribe. Job lived until the fourth generation of his sons and grandsons despite the loss of his ten first children.

What can explain the suffering of a Christian? How did the famous Christians, especially heroes of the Bible, perceive the hardship they were going through? Let's look at some cases according to the Scriptures:

> *«Blessed are you when men shall revile you and persecute you, and shall say all kinds of evil against you falsely, for My sake. **Rejoice and be exceedingly glad, for your reward in heaven is great**. For so they persecuted the prophets who were before you»* (**Matthew 5:11-12**).

Through these verses, the Lord warns the Christian that he will suffer persecution because of His name. The Christian should not be surprised if the environment in which he lives becomes hostile. He must accept it in the calmness and hope, like Apostles of the following narration, after being outraged by the Pharisees:

> *«And calling the Apostles, beating them, they commanded not to speak in the name of Jesus, and let them go. Then indeed they departed from the presence of the Sanhedrin, **rejoicing that they were counted worthy to be shamed for His name**»* (**Acts 5:40-41**).

It is surprising that instead of pestering against their aggressors, these heroes of the Bible declared themselves ***rejoicing that they were counted worthy to be shamed for Jesus name***. They were happy and not desperate. It is an indicator of sanctification. Yet these apostles did not yet justify a long experience in Christianity because Jesus had been with them only three years before ascending to heaven. So they had barely four years of Christian life at the time of these events.

> «***But I (Jesus) say to you, do not resist evil****. But whoever shall strike you on your right cheek, **turn the other to him also***. And to him desiring to sue you, and to take away your tunic, **let him have your coat also***. And whoever shall compel you to go a mile, go with him two»* (**Matthew 5:39-41**).

Through these verses, the Lord invites the Christian to give up fighting with the flesh. Jesus goes even further by saying, "*If anyone desires to come after Me, let him deny himself and take up his cross and follow Me*" (**Matthew 16:24**).

One has the impression that Jesus encouraged His disciples to suffer while suffering is never desired. Jesus

Christ Himself did not love the Cross He carried to Golgotha. This Cross was imposed upon him. However, Jesus accepted it without murmuring.

Jesus does not encourage His Christians to desire suffering, rather to endure it without murmuring. We can always wonder why we must turn the second cheek, give the second tunic and go one more mile than we are compelled to? Apart from Jesus' call to accept the suffering, the answer to this question is implicit. It shines through the Scriptures.

Suffering as a shield against devil's actions

The devil knows that it takes time for the Christian to sanctify himself and acquire the humility that God expects. Therefore he knows that the Christian continues to maintain some inner pride inherited from the world he comes from. There is nothing better for the devil than to undermine the pride of this Christian hoping that the latter will fight, not to mention taking shortcuts where the devil intends to attack. For the devil knows that sin offers a privileged ground for causing serious damage to Christians, such as the death he brought to the human race by seducing Adam and Eve. The devil knows that God truly hates sin. His usual strategy has always been to compromise man in a sin that will draw him the wrath of God. He thus rides on this divine wrath to perpetrate damage on the Christian's life.

This is where the problem of many Christians lies. They do not want to be ashamed in front of the world. It is a window that the devil exploits to paralyze the spiritual life of many Christians. The devil compromises them in bad postures. What will the Christian do in a negative spiral of life? How many Christians take shortcuts to get by? The devil relies on the Christian's dislike for shame and suffering to bring him to a slippery floor; and even he secretly hopes that the Christian will come to an agreement with him to arrange his commodities of life.

Here is the answer of the Lord: **the Christian must accept the dishonor of Christ on his life**. If he must go through humiliation and hardship, he should bear it and sin no more. In general, hardship will only last a time, and then he will come out victor.

Let us remember that Abraham faced the humiliation of losing his wife Sara twice because of a persistent famine that drove him out of his land. He lost Sara for the benefit of the Egypt Pharaoh the first time, and for the benefit of the king of Gerar, the second time. Each time he got out of trouble without cursing God.

Did Job have to go into debt to maintain his pride as the richest man in the East, and hide the fact that poverty was knocking at his door? Dear Christian, are you going on consecutive initiatives to escape a negative spiral? Relax and accept the Stations of the Cross offered to you as Job. The latter does not compromise to hide his social condition continuously degrading, far from its opulence of prime.

When the Christian has accepted the fate that God proposes him, the devil has no longer any argument to make, except to wait for the Christian, tired of suffering, to crack and sin. If that does not happen, it's the devil's failure. A resounding failure like the resurrection of Christ that he did not expect.

It is because the devil, himself, has never faced degradation before God sentencing him for life in hell. He was adorned, from his creation, with all kinds of precious jewels, with a splendor unparalleled in the creation of God. The devil has never adopted an attitude of humility. He only knows that to avoid going through humiliation and losing face, you must try everything, legally or illegally. The main thing is to avoid deprivation at all costs. When the Christian resorts to illegality, the devil enjoys the opportunity to cause great harm in his life.

Suffering is therefore a method of teaching that the Lord uses to protect Christians from the wiles of the devil.

The Christian triumphs over shame and mockery

We must insist on the question of shame and say that Christians should not make it an obstacle to sanctification. Many Christians continue to be ashamed for one reason or another. But the Christian is a new creature whose life before conversion was covered by the blood of the Lamb. He no longer has to be ashamed of this past to go forward in Christianity.

Apostle Paul was persecuting the church of Jesus Christ before becoming a Christian. He recorded the death of one of the most famous martyrs of the emerging Christian era, the deacon Stephen (**Acts 8:1**). Can we see in the writings of this prolific apostle any mark of shame? No at all. Paul's writings are full of vivacity and exhortation to progress in sanctification. The apostle was not ashamed to appear before the Christians he formerly persecuted, nor before the clergy who had formerly sent him against these same Christians.

If there is no reason to be ashamed of his past life, the Christian do not have to be indefinitely ashamed of the blunders he commits in his new life. The Lord asks him to confess his sins and he will be forgiven (**1John 1:9**). To maintain remorse instead of repenting that the Bible recommends, can lead the Christian into a negative spiral, from bad to worse. Let us remember King David after committing adultery with the wife of one of his generals. To hide his crime, he devised a ploy to impute the adulterous pregnancy to the abused general. Not succeeding, he resolved to put an end to the general's life. This episode triggered a succession of tragedies that God allowed in retaliation. Not only did two of David's sons die in the prime of life, but also one of them led a coup against his father, forced to return to power by means of a fratricidal war.

The opportunity given to the Christian to be purified by the blood of Christ is an immense grace because we know how much the soul guilt after the fault. Some go through deep depression. Thanks to the blood of Jesus Christ, the Christian can atone for his fault and find his vivacity and peace. This opportunity for forgiveness is truly a grace of the Lord. The Christian is not asked to judge the legitimacy of grace, as a prisoner does not have to judge the presidential pardon that liberates him. The Christian is forgiven, that's all. The Holy Spirit he received at conversion is the evidence of it.

I insist again on the need for the Christian not to make shame an obstacle to his sanctification. May I be allowed to declare, through these lines, that the Lord often resorts to shame to develop a sense of humility in the Christian's life. As such, the Christian is invited not to fight against the false accusations he will often be the object of. No matter whether he is right or wrong, the Lord will recommend to him the silence and shame that goes with it. Since silence in front of a charge looks like consent, the Christian is often invited to accept this disgraceful role even if he is not the real culprit. His silence can have the effect, at first, of cooling a climate of rising tension. It is in a peaceful situation that the Christian will be able to expose his truth – if it is really necessary. Often it will not be long for people to realize that the Christian has been wrongly accused. It is the Lord who, proud of the attitude of humility of the Christian, creates the conditions for his rehabilitation. The Lord will then reach two goals. First He has developed the gift of humility in the Christian, and second, has restored the Christian in his right to the shame of the enemy. *"Not avenging yourselves, beloved, but giving place to wrath; for it is written, 'Vengeance is Mine, I will repay', says the lord."* (**Romans 12:19**). Anger can rise when one is accused wrongly. The situation is obviously very uncomfortable when all eyes are on you. But the Lord is firm: *Vengeance is Mine, I will repay.* He is the Avenger of the Christian. This is the burden of the Christian in the world. He will be ashamed but the Lord will restore him.

The case of Joseph, sold by his brothers and ending governor of Egypt; Daniel, wrongly accused and thrown into the lions' den without being scratched, are there to give credibility to the recommendation above.

Dear Christians, do not be afraid of shame to the point of compromising your sanctification. Repent of your sins quickly, even if for that you should be ashamed. On the spot the shame is painful. But in the end, we are relieved to have freed our soul from a terrible burden. The enemy wants to trap the unstable Christians in the hope that shame will make them stumble as King David in his desire to conceal adultery.

By the Spirit that dwells in him, the Christian is strongly equipped and able to bear the shame of Christ in all the situations he will go through.

The virtues of suffering in Christ

> *«It is good for me that I have been afflicted, so that I might learn your precepts»* **Psalms 119:71**.

Imagine the young boy about to be circumcised. He is afraid and it is normal. Will mom spare him circumcision because he is afraid? No! She will have him circumcised because of the virtues of the circumcision, whether the boy agrees or not.

The same goes with Christians who suffer. The Christian is afraid of suffering. Nothing more normal. But will the Lord spare him? No, because of the virtues of suffering for this Christian.

The Lord has made it clear, and repeatedly, that *whoever does not bear his cross and come after Him, he cannot be His disciple.* (**Luke 14:27**). This verse and others alike leave no doubt that Christians will suffer. But when one analyzes Christians' behavior, many of them associate suffering with an active sin or curse. Job's three friends went this direction to explain the old man's misfortunes at the twilight of his life. For them, Job was a malefactor whose dissolute life was exposed to the face of the world. We know that God severely reprimanded these critics and made it known to the three pretentious (**Job 40:7-9**).

Did Job sin before going through all the misfortunes that struck him? Was it about an unbroken curse? Nothing at all. God tested His servant and appreciated the result. Hence the reward that God gave him, twice what he had lost before (**Job 42:10**).

The memory of Job is regularly recalled by Apostles to explain the suffering of Christians. They explained that whoever does not know the suffering is a bastard, and that God corrects those He loves, as the below Scriptures tell:

*«But when we are judged, we are chastened by the Lord, **that we should not be condemned with the world**»* (**1 Corinthians 11:32**).

*«**For whom the Lord loves He chastens, and He scourges every son whom He receives**. If you endure chastening, God deals with you as with sons, for what son is he whom the father does not chasten? (…) For truly our fathers chastened us for a few days according to their own pleasure, but **God for our profit, that we might be partakers of His holiness**»* (**Hebrews 12:6-7; 10**).

*«As many as I (Jesus) love, **I rebuke and chasten**; therefore be zealous and repent»* (**Revelation 3:19**)

May Christians stop crying and blaming themselves in the midst of tribulation. May they remain in recollection and praise to God. Although God approved Job throughout his drama, the latter multiplied questions, sometimes daring, about God who, according to Job, let fate go on him – Job did not sin because he glorified God nonetheless (**Job 1:20-22**). But God asks us to be perfect by avoiding murmuring. Job had no antecedent to rely on to understand his misfortunes, so he kept on questioning. As today's Christians know the story of Job, they have no excuse for systematically putting their misfortunes on their past and imagined sins. Job, like other heroes of the Bible, is a model Christians can draw inspiration from to maintain an attitude of dignity, recollection and adoration in all their tribulations – this is the cross promised by the Lord for every Christian.

I must make a fundamental point here. If a Christian sins, he will be punished unless he repents as the Bible exhorts him. If the Christian does not repent, he will go through suffering. The Bible makes it very accurate from Genesis to Revelation. After repentance, the corrective suffering should normally stop. The Christian must not tolerate vain suffering – often sustained by the devil. The Christian must demand his healing after repentance. God is not a man to rage for a long time, like humans, in proportioning the correction to the fault. God forgives and relieves without ulterior motive.

If a Christian believes that his problems have something to do with any sin, and after deep repentance, the problem still persists, let him not panic. It may be a divine trial initiated for one's good, such as Apostle Paul, attained in his flesh to remind him of the virtues of humility and divine grace (**2 Corinthians 12:7-9**). May the Christian persevere in vigilance, meditation and adoration. Apostle Peter evoked this cruel episode of the Christian life by exhorting with these words: "*Let none of you suffer as a murderer, or a thief, or an evildoer, or a meddler in the affairs of others. But if one suffers as a Christian, let him not be ashamed, but **let him glorify God because of this**"*(**1 Peter 4:15-16**).

I can testify to many of these ordeals that I have personally endured. God ends up consoling you unrelated to losses suffered during the ordeal. God rewards you a hundredfold for what you lose because of His name, so much so that you may be pushed to caress suffering – a folly that I do not recommend. I note however that by virtue of his piety, Apostle Paul had to free himself from the material comfort gospel gave him the right to. He avoided for example getting married. He refused the gifts of Corinthians. He made many recommendations in this direction for those who aspired to high quality sanctification – without making it a commandment as some less inspired Christians do at their expense.

It is sad that Christians hold absolutely to impute to any sin the misfortunes that afflict them. It is a mistake to do so. Despite exhortations calling for restraint, some Christians persist in this posture. These are Christians the Bible treats as irresolute: these Christians will get nothing back. They believe that being a Christian means the end of problems and the beginning of an Eldorado on Earth. This is not the message of Jesus Christ's Gospel. No way.

I invite Christians presently in an endless suffering, unrelated to a known sin, not to feel guilty, but to maintain an attitude of recollection with thanksgiving for the Lord. It will last as long as the Lord decides regardless of the Christian's opinion. The happy ending will be beyond hope, *good measure pressed down and shaken together and running over* (**Luke 6:38**).

If a Christian does not accept this teaching, let him stop overwhelming pastors and the Christian community. The Bible says of this Christian that he is irresolute and undisciplined, that he will get nothing (**James 1:8**). The time of God remains the one imposed by God. No complaint will change anything.

Are you in touch with a long lasting and painful situation that does not seem to work out? Welcome to the sheepfold of Christ! Rejoice to be a Christian because it is to them that it happens most often. Do you have difficulty repeatedly, seemingly insurmountable? Do not panic. Rather, rejoice and glorify God (**1 Peter 4:16**). I say: rejoice! For this is the reason why the Lord made you His Christian. The devil is trying to rot your life to force you to betray the beautiful name of Christ. Do not follow him in this way, but rejoice. In contrast to Job, who bore the suffering by scolding a few times, you were sealed by the Holy Spirit when you believed, a Special Equipment for Christians to support everything in meditation and joy. The Scriptures recommend it.

> «***Rejoicing in hope***, *patient in affliction, steadfastly continuing in prayer*» (**Romans 12:12***)*.

> «***Rejoice*** *with rejoicing ones, and weep with weeping ones*» (**Romans 12:15***)*.

> ***«Rejoice, O nations, with His people»*** **(Romans 15:10)**.

> *«And you also **rejoice in the same, and rejoice with me»*** **(Philippians 2:18)**.

> *«Finally, my brothers, **rejoice in the Lord»*** **(Philippians 3:1)**.

> ***«Rejoice in the lord always. Again I say, rejoice!»*** **(Philippians 4:4)**.

> *«But **rejoice according as you are partakers of Christ's suffering**, so that when His glory shall be revealed, you may be glad also with exceeding joy»* **(1 Peter 4:13)**.

> *«Therefore **rejoice, O heavens, and those tabernacling in them»*** **(Revelation 12:12)**.

All these calls to rejoice may surprise. In fact, to see closely and observing the joy of the mother in front of her baby, it is no longer astonishing that the Lord rejoices every time he sees a Christian, fruit of His sacrifice on the cross. While rejoicing in spite of your difficulties, you teach a great lesson of humility and wisdom to the enemy, who realizes that he has lost his war against you.

Suffering in Christ triumphs over boasting and childish imagination

Regarding the last days, Apostle Paul prophesized in these terms:

> «*In the last days* **grievous times will be at hand***. For men will be self-lovers, money-lovers, boasters, proud, blasphemers, disobedient to parents, unthankful, unholy, without natural affection, unyielding, false accusers, without self-control, savage, despisers of good, traitors, reckless, puffed up, lovers of pleasure rather than lovers of God, having a form of godliness, but denying the power of it; even turn away from these*» (**2 Timothy 3:1-5**).

Looking around, doesn't anyone feel like we're almost there? People are turning away from the truth despite reminders to order. We rush to ephemeral pleasures, then feel a vacuum that grows as we try to fill it. More and more, the piety of the children of God is experienced as an agony by them. It is here that they will need a real comforter. The Holy Spirit is that Comforter they need more than ever. More importantly, in addition to consolation, the Holy Spirit will grow in them the joy that this world cannot offer despite the explosion of artificial creativity – Internet and digital gadgets.

The fear expressed by the Lord Jesus Christ in His time is here already: *Will Christians still have faith in these times of the end?* Behold the shield against the increasing unbelief and illusions of the flesh: the Holy Spirit.

Let us remember that the Christian life can't be commanded or imagined: it is lived. Not only Sundays of praising His Heavenly Majesty, which God appreciates enormously, but also every day, twenty-four hours a day. Let the Christian stop imagining the Christian life as an Eldorado on earth – the Eldorado will come in its time, on a new earth with new heavens, so be patient – for we are not there yet; let him live his Christendom thoroughly, otherwise his Sunday praise will pass for that of the lips God condemned among the Israelites of the Old Covenant.

What we are saying is that the Word of God should not be flayed. It clearly announces that *all who desire to live godly in Christ Jesus will be persecuted* (**2 Timothy 3:12**). In addition Jesus Christ called every Christian *to deny himself and take up his cross and follow Him* (**Matthew 16:24**), which predestines the Christian to suffer. Yes and three times yes, the cross announced by Jesus Christ carries a word in it: suffering. Do not pretend to ignore it. Where is the problem when a Christian suffers? Why so much panic? Why self-inventing all kinds of stories about sins that would have been committed? Jesus recommends repentance in case of sin. If a Christian has sinned, let him repent and the Lord will forgive him without hesitation. I say without hesitation because He promised to do so, and Apostles confirm it (**1 John 1: 9**). To mourn with remorse and guilt suits the doing of this world, it is paganism and paganism is flesh. The Christian walks *according to the Spirit and not according to the flesh because if he walks according to the flesh, he will die* (**Romans 8:13**).

Jesus calls Christians to rejoice when these sufferings occur because it is the evidence that they are Christians (**Matthew 5:3-12**). Suffering will occur even in opulence. No Christian can escape. Many Christians pray to get their problems solved. They are right. The Lord has promised to deliver them. But what they need to know is that the Lord has not promised a specific timetable for ending the crisis, and that they must not imagine it is because of a sin that they are afflicted. It's a pagan thought. If they are aware of having sinned, let them repent and the Lord will forgive them. So they do not have to panic when problems persist. The Christian does not have to define his standard of the bearable. If the Christian does it, he deceives himself. He invents an imaginary world that is not Bible's, but personal, selfish and carnal. The endurable of the Christian is no longer human, but divine because it is God who controls the situation. Many Christians live in humanly inextricable situations, sufferings that they do not usually see around them. That they do not panic because the Lord is more jealous than a mother to her baby. The Lord is jealous for this Christian He cherishes more than anything. How will He let the Christian down where a mother, a mere creature of Him, cannot? It is failure in basic faith to think so. May the Christian not panic. Apostle Peter advised him to move away from evil and do good, to seek peace and to pursue it (**1 Peter 3:11**). May he remain in godliness and he will see the glory of God. This glory will not differ because that is what defines God. A God without glory, what would it be? God presented Himself to Moses with great glory. It's His habit. He never changes. He will show His glory to His believer – the Christian.

In fact, the suffering of the Christian no longer belongs to him. Just like his life. Apostle Paul made it known at the time saying, "***None of us lives to himself, and no one dies to himself.*** *For both if we live, we live to the Lord; and if we die, we die to the Lord.* ***Therefore both if we live, and if we die, we are the Lord's***" (**Romans 14:7-8**).

Isn't that great? What are people of the world afraid of? Suffering, death and woes. It is because they feel responsible for their lives that they are afraid of misusing it and ending up as they would not have liked. The Christian must rejoice because he NO LONGER HAS TO worry about his life as if he were the owner of it. For indeed: ***None of us lives to himself, and no one dies to himself.*** The Owner who now responds to the life of the Christian is the Lord Jesus Christ. Hence the call to relax. Christians should not stress like the people of the world who gnaw their souls with worry. The Christian is rather relaxed. Amen.

The Christian's victory is not based on strength, wisdom or wealth

In front of Goliath, David made this statement:

> «*You come to me with a sword and with a spear and with a javelin*. *But I come to you in the name of Jehovah of hosts, the God of the armies of Israel, Whom you have defied. (...) All this multitude shall know that **Jehovah does not save with sword and spear; for the battle is Jehovah's, and He will give you into our hands**»* (1 Samuel 17:45-47).

The triumph of the children of God is not based on strength, wisdom or wealth. This statement certainly goes against human thinking where victory is a matter of intelligence, cunning, effort, money, material means, determination and other similar things.

It is shocking to hear that we can conquer and triumph without these elements. Oh yes! God does not need

Christians' wisdom, wealth and strength to take on adversity. Because **it is He who fights for them**. One could well imagine that teenager David, the slingshot and the stone could not, alone, defeat Goliath, a so experienced warrior since his childhood. Just as Moses could not, with his intelligence, cross the Red Sea as he did on the dry land, between two arms of sea. It is doubtful that the people of Israel could defeat the fearsome realms on the way of the promised land, only thanks to his military genius. God was at work. He is at work today to lead the fighting of Christians in place of these, provided that Christians trust him.

I measure the difficulty of understanding this chapter if we have not put it into practice. How to bring a Christian to free himself from the know-how that has accompanied him since his birth, from relying on financial, material and intellectual means in the face of adversity? This is the challenge of this chapter. But I repeat it again, only the practice will make understand and figure out what is said in this chapter. Only practice has led me to understand it, to speak about it in these lines. Does Apostle Paul not say: "*I have been crucified with Christ, and **I live; yet no longer I, but Christ lives in me**. And that life I now live in the flesh, I live by faith toward the Son of God, who loved me and gave Himself on my behalf*"(**Galatians 2:20**)?

What's up with *Christ lives in me*? We mean that from now on, the Christian must consider his upper and lower limbs as those of Christ, as well as his body, his health, his abilities, his savoir-faire and know-how. As such, the Christian must sanctify himself every day so that the Holy Spirit finds pleasure in acting through him. In case of non-active sanctification, Christ will not show in the Christian. It will be said of this Christian that the Holy Spirit is extinguished in him. The Holy Spirit has not left him. He's just turned off.

A practical case concerns the workplace. Going to work means coming with Christ at the workplace. The Christian must be aware of this invisible but true reality. The less fervent Christian does not suspect anything, but in reality Christ is very active in the Christian's workplace. Depending on the level of sanctification, Christ can harden the boss's heart against the Christian (if the Lord wants to correct the Christian) or direct the heart of that boss in favor of the Christian (if the Lord will rather reward him). The pagans will suspect nothing, but the Christian will be aware of the activity of the Lord wherever he goes: workplace, grocery, bakery, supermarket, hospital, public services, toilet, etc.

Once again, the words above will sound empty in the eyes of the Christian who does not put these into practice to figure out this reality. It is by practicing that the heroes of the Bible and the Christians of today have perfectly figured out how *"Christ lives in them"* (**Galatians 2:20**).

Let's meditate again on the following Bible verses:

> **«*Do not yield your members as instruments of unrighteousness to sin*, but yield yourselves to God, as one alive from the dead, *and your members as instruments of righteousness to God*»** (**Romans 6:13**).

> «*If the Spirit of the One who raised up Jesus from the dead dwells in you, the One who raised up Christ from the dead **shall also make your mortal bodies alive by His spirit who dwells in you***» (**Romans 8:11**).

> «*Do you not know that **your bodies are the members of Christ?** Shall I then take the members of Christ and make them the members of a harlot?*» (**1 Corinthians 6:15**).

The arms of the Christian – head, hands, feet – and the rest of the body now belong to Christ as **1 Corinthians 6:15** emphasizes above. The Christian must be aware of this reality and draw all the consequences, even if this reality is invisible to him. The Christian's strength lies in the fact that he trusts God before seeing anything happens. Such is the Christian's faith, the one defined by the Bible.

According to **Romans 8:11**, although our members are growing old because of the death decree pronounced in Eden Garden, they can receive the life of the Spirit for the service of God, like David slaying Goliath.

I want to make the following point: God is not against national education, on the contrary. The national education system, with its programs and exams, is very useful to humanity. God has made these tools available to the pagans who do not know Him. On the other hand, God asks Christians to trust Him. Can the Christian also use these tools of national education? Yes absolutely. We support in this chapter that the Christian has **a better quality tool** to overcome adversity: **faith in God** provided the Christian implements it. Without practice, the words of this chapter are just empty writings and senseless; and the Christian will see to his shame, people like Joseph – son of Jacob – governing a powerful country without going through the local degree system. He will see people like Daniel – the deported – use the wisdom of God to govern a powerful country, without going through the local degree system. It is the same with David: he did not use the conventional weapons of war to defeat General Goliath.

The obedient Christian must therefore expect God – who lives in him – to reach His righteousness in the world through him.

The Christian triumphs over the seduction of money

> *«Therefore do not be anxious, saying, what shall we eat? Or, what shall we drink? Or, with what shall we be clothed? For the nations seek after all these things. For your heavenly Father knows that you have need of all these things. But seek first the kingdom of God and His righteousness; and all these things shall be added to you. Therefore do not be anxious about tomorrow; for tomorrow shall be anxious for its own things. Sufficient to the day is the evil of it»* **Matthew 6:31-34**.

Does God recommend that Christians live without money? No, that is not the purpose of this chapter. We cannot speak of the triumph of Christians without mentioning how they relate to money, the *sinews of war*. Apostle Paul declares that *the love of money is the root of all evil*. Let's get to the point. Do you think the Lord ignores the saying *whoever pays decides*? How will the Lord Jesus Christ maintain His authority over the Christian if He does not rule the vital resources the Christian's dependent of? How will the Lord impose His lordship on the Christian when the latter has a different boss who feeds him? The boss in this world would he not blackmail to force the Christian to abandon Christ?

Whoever pays decides

Men are used to submit to anyone feeds them. Slaves are submitted to their masters for this reason. Workers are submitted to bosses for monthly salaries. In fact, who does not pay, cannot command or decide. How will the Lord Jesus Christ maintain His lordship and authority over the Christian who does not depend on Him for his daily bread? To leave this question unanswered is to weaken His authority over the Christian. The Lord Jesus Christ cannot leave this question unsolved. This is the reason for His message to Christians so that they may become attached to Him. If the Lord had left such a void, Satan would have occupied it to become, in the long run, the true master of Christians. Men are not fooled. They all give honor and fidelity to whoever feeds them. Thus the royal dynasties forged family names. This is because a patriarch of this family had, in the past, provided protection for men, women and their goods.

Christ is the only One who feeds Christians

The above principle being said, we must declare that the Christian can no longer have on earth any provider other than the Lord Jesus Christ. The Christian must now be aware that the only provider of his daily bread on the earth is the Lord. The Christian is a privileged one of God, an heir of grace, co-heir with Christ on the throne of God, a loved one with the Holy Spirit in him. From the moment he became a Christian, he shifted from the world of darkness to the world of light because "*God has delivered us from the power of darkness and has translated us into the kingdom of His dear Son*" (**Colossians 1:13**). God could not leave the question of the Christian's daily bread in abeyance. He could not leave the Christian at the mercy of the unknown with regard to his daily bread, clothing and lodging. The Lord really takes this question seriously in the lives of His Christians.

From now on, the Christian pursues a life of sanctification where nothing escapes from the Lord. The Lord will ensure that the daily bread of the Christian is assured. The Christian should not be surprised to find out that the Lord is involved in his living regarding this fundamental question. Many Christians, serving the Lord in the world, have testified to the Lord's favorable and decisive hand in the way they are fed. From the conversion and baptism of the Christian, there is no transition period between his dependence on the world he has just left, and his dependence on the Lord he has just joined. It is very quickly that the Christian is taken care by the Lord.

Concretely it is very difficult, we agree, but in true, the Lord cannot leave this question unanswered because the world will try to blackmail the Christian to get him far away from Christ. The Christian must bear in mind that in case of a clash with the world, up to his job dismissal, Jesus Christ will take care of him. Needless to imagine how it will happen. The Lord alone knows how He will proceed. This is the commitment He has made to the Christian: He will not fail.

Speaking of how, many believe that to depend completely on God for eating and drinking, means to work full time for the church. This perception of things is completely wrong. It is true that groups of Christians, according to their heavenly vocation, have illustrated their devotion by working full time in the church. This is specific to these Christians but cannot be extended to all Christians. The word of God makes possible specific vows to God, which can affect earthly goods, working time and other achievements of life. But such a wish depends on the personal choice of this Christian. He is not authorized to make it a standard that will divide Christians between adherents and non-adherents, super and moderately sanctified Christians. It is unfortunate that churches have not paid enough attention to these sources of division to the point where there are Christians more committed than others, those who carry the burden and those who are mere church goers – spectators. Some personal arrangements in the Christian's life are often merely symbolic, without contributing to holiness. The word of God says it many times. Apostle Paul, himself, has not made of his personal arrangements, the model to popularize such as, for example, not to marry. Depending on circumstances, he could work as a tents weaver for his daily bread or depend on contributions from afar. He will sometimes send serious warnings to Christians who preached not to marry, and to Christians who did not want to work.

Whether the Christian is full-time or part-time church worker, or is a world's company worker, his salary comes from the Lord God. It is God who uses his boss to assure him his daily bread. God knows the amount that He can change at will, up and down, or even end his job in a company. The work of a Christian in any company must be considered a work done for the Lord. For this job is sanctified by the Christian. This work contributes to his food which is a major concern of the Lord: taking care of the Christian. It is therefore perilous for the Christian to neglect the job of a company on the pretext that this job does not directly serve God, or that his colleagues are pagans. This Christian is totally mistaken. The Lord has eyes everywhere. More importantly, He wants every job done in the world to be executed to perfection. Indeed, Christians know how to be generous and exhibit their holiness in the church alongside other Christians. Well, God knows this carnal tendency of Christians! He will want to appreciate this Christian in his workplace, when other Christians do not look at him. If he is careless in the world and serious in the church, his sanctification will not be accepted by the Lord because of his hypocrisy. The Lord also says, "*Let your light so shine before men that they may see your good works and glorify your Father who is in heaven*" (**Matthew 5:16**). The Christian cannot neglect a job done in the world, for fear of discrediting his Father who is in heaven.

We recapitulate by saying that once born again, the Christian depends exclusively on God for his daily bread that is eating, drinking, dressing and lodging, even if, to do so, the Lord can use various means like job or other resources. The question is not how the Lord will proceed, but to fix our gaze on Christ who promised these things with assurance: *Do not be anxious about tomorrow; for Tomorrow shall be anxious for its own things. Sufficient to the day is the evil of it* (**Matthew 6: 31-34**). *As the hart pants after the water brooks, so my soul pants after You, O god* (**Psalm 42:1**).

The Christian must think seriously at his daily bread because this area is where the most corruption is recorded. It is very easy to blackmail and buy one soul who depends on others to survive, as it is easy for the soul to submit to the one who feeds him. The Christian must understand that his soul, so dear to God, will never belong to anyone else but God. The soul of the Christian is as dear to God as targeted by the devil. The devil would greatly appreciate having under him a soul saved by the Lord

(Christian). Why? First, to boast of having sons of light working for him and eating in his hand. Secondly because Christians have blessings that the devil is eager to grab. What could be more beautiful for him than to lay hands on sanctified goods! Therefore, a Christian's source of income must absolutely glorify the Lord. A Christian who neglects the sanctification of his resources will soon be targeted by the devil who wants to compromise him. What a joy for the devil if he could proclaim to anyone that he feeds Christians! A negligence of the Christian, on the sanctification of his resources, will lead him to blaspheme the glorious name of the Lord. In practice, it is impossible for these trials not to happen. Christians will sometimes face threats to their jobs, careers and social status. To the question *What will I become if I lose this job?* The Lord replies: *Do not be anxious about tomorrow; for Tomorrow shall be anxious for its own things. Sufficient to the day is the evil of it*. The next day will worry about himself. Finally, the Christian in difficulty must never indicate, by an external posture (unhappy look, ragged clothes,

> hesitant step, etc.), that he is weak and needs help. **The Christian is not a beggar**. God knows everything about this Christian, when he goes out and comes in, when he sleeps and wakes up, when he laughs and cries. He knows everything he has in his attic. The Lord will be able to interact in a timely manner. It's hard but you have to believe it and the Lord will confirm His word. The Lord knows that the Christian is the light of the world. He will not do anything contradictory.

If the lack of money deeply influences your temperament and your posture, then you are not out of his grip. The devil and his collaborators still have a way of blackmail you. If salary delays and financial difficulties make you lose peace, then you are in the same situation. God wants His child to discover for himself that he is not risking anything. This is easy to say than to do, I recognize it. But who said that faith is practiced without anxiety or stress? Anxiety and stress are part of the daily life of the Christian because God is invisible. The Christian, like every human being, bears better a situation of danger when accompanied by another visible person; but behold, God is invisible and wishes to be trustworthy as if He were visible. Faith is at this price.

To deliver the Christian from the awful hold of money, in addition to the above advice, God will put the Christian in humanly uncomfortable situations, which will make this Christian think that God has abandoned him. This situation may get worse when some Christians, like the three friends of Job, will try to convince him that his problems originate from a hidden life full of sins and wrong doings.

In such situations, the Christian must stand firm in dignity and faith, and he will see the glory of God. Whatever disastrous situation he will go through, God will be in control and will prove to him that he has never abandoned him, never.

The Christian triumphs over fashion

We must recognize that good manners are also sources of prejudices and discriminations in this world. Thus the populations of the big cities consider those of the other cities as barbarians, wild, ignorant, rough and manner-less. Jesus Himself was accused of being from a gloomy city of Nazareth in Galilee, of eating with tax collectors, of not washing hands before meals. All these good manners are pretty to see. At a time when absolute monarchies dominated the world, each social class was distinguished by a dress code in addition to bodily gestures of courtesy. But for the Lord, these rituals and good manners are not primordial anymore. Christians are called to free themselves from their tyranny. Do you eat at times not indicated by human tradition? No problem. Do you want to celebrate God outside of the dedicated days of worship? Feel free. Do you want to eat meat when the vegetarian diet is de rigueur? Feel free. Have you been told that you need to apply a precautionary measure before you commit? Go for it! The Lord will be with you. *Where the Spirit of the Lord is, there is freedom.* Have you been told that such food is favorable or unfavorable in this context? Let be guided by the Spirit and not by good manners. You are first of all the crown princes of the kingdom of heaven. Apostle Paul had already rebelled against the tyranny of these traditions. He said for example:

> *«But now, knowing God, but rather are known by God, **how do you turn again to the weak and beggarly elements to which you again desire to slave anew? You observe days and months and times and years**. I fear for you, lest somehow I have labored among you in vain. Brothers, I beseech you, be as I am; for I am as you»* (**Galatians 4:9-12**).

Sometimes, good manners have the unacknowledged purpose of subjugating docile and fragile people. It is a shame to find these shameful doings in the Church of Jesus Christ. Apostle Paul rebelled against these methods in harsh terms as follows:

> *«**For you endure if anyone enslaves you, if anyone devours, if anyone takes from you, if anyone exalts himself, if anyone strikes you in the face**. I speak according to dishonor»* (**2 Corinthians 11:20-21**).

Christians are free because Jesus has set them truly free. Amen.

The Christian triumphs over the barriers of science

As citizens of the kingdom of heaven, Christians should not be surprised to experience situations rarely mentioned in the world. Good or bad inextricable situations will happen to them. The kingdom of heavens being different from the earth, Christians should not be surprised that the laws of science could often not prevail where they live. By multiplying bread, turning water into wine, walking on water, Jesus showed that the laws of science are pointless compared to the kingdom of heavens. That is, the laws of science could lose their effects on Christians.

In interrupting the storm, Jesus was also showing that He was more competent than all the weather stations on earth. The latter can at best predict a storm, but we have never heard that a weather station had interrupted a storm like Jesus did.

Christians must not lock themselves into human boundaries of knowledge. Let them stop suffering because the Lord is above science.

The Christian triumphs over the worship of holy days, holy places and holy meals

The man is naturally inclined towards religion. Many believe that this tendency is to fill the void left in the spirit of our ancestors Adam and Eve after the Fall. It is however a reality that the human being tends to develop a religious activity. He is superstitious. This explains why, despite the call of Jesus and His disciples not to erect holy days, places and meals, Christians persist in doing so. Let's see what Jesus said in His time:

> «*The hour is coming when you shall neither worship the Father in this mountain nor yet at Jerusalem. (...) But the hour is coming, and now is, when **the true worshipers shall worship the Father in spirit and truth**, for the Father seeks such to worship Him. God is a spirit, and they who worship Him must worship in spirit and in truth*» (**John 4:21-24**).

According to the Law of Moses, every Jew had to pray the face turned towards the holy city of Jerusalem. Commemorations under the Law could only be done in Jerusalem. Therefore, these solemnities were occasions for regrouping Jews from diaspora in Jerusalem. In addition to the holy place of Jerusalem, the days of the said commemorations were also holy days.

But Jesus came to announce that the earthly Jerusalem was no longer a holy city in the eyes of God the Father, nor any other place on earth. Apostle Paul drives the point by comparing this earthly Jerusalem to the spiritual figure of Hagar, the slave of Sarah (**Galatians 4:25**). For Jesus, the worshipers His Father seeks – the spiritual sons of Sarah – are the ones who worship the Father in spirit and in truth. Thus Jesus released his Christians from the tyranny of the holy places and days to which, alas for their misfortunes, the spiritual sons of Hagar – the inhabitants of the earthly Jerusalem – continue to submit.

Jesus has in fact released Christians from all tyrannies, including that of holy meals. When asked about it, Apostle Paul answered:

> « *I know, and am persuaded by the Lord Jesus, that **there is nothing unclean of itself**: but to him that esteemeth any thing to be unclean, to him it is unclean*» (**Romans 14:14/ Bible 1769 Authorized Version**).

> «*Therefore **let no one judge you in food or in drink, or in respect of a feast, or of the new moon, or of the sabbaths***.

For these are a shadow of things to come, but the body is of Christ (**Colossians 2:16-17**).

*«If then you died with Christ from the elements of the world, **why, as though living in the world, are you subject to its ordinances: Touch not, taste not, handle not**; which things are all for corruption in the using, according to the commands and doctrines of men? These things indeed have a reputation of wisdom in self-imposed worship and humility, and unsparing severity of the body, **but are not of any value** for the satisfying of the flesh»* (**Colossians 2:20-23**).

The Christian is thus released from the worship of holy days, holy places and holy meals.

Concretely, you can eat pork when people around consider it impure, while avoiding to provoke them – do it thus in private. You can eat beef in a world of vegetarians.

For the sake of the weak, however, he who esteems holy a day, a place or a meal, let him do it freely for God, without making others suffer, to avoid unnecessary conflicts.

The Lord knows that appearances are deceptive. What distinguishes a true Christian from a sorcerer disguised as a Christian? Nothing. Both can be confused. By getting rid of the tyranny of holy days, places and meals, the Lord is allowing us to live relaxed and free. He no longer wants caricatures of worshipers, mountain and caves worshipers. He wants worshipers in spirit and in truth for His Father.

The Christian triumphs over sin

Needless to say how important this theme is in the Christian community. How many Christians struggle against sins that haunt them day after day, and that they do not know how to get rid of? How many Christians succumb to a recurring sin? Many, even though they keep it secret, just like the little child who, after pissing on his clothes, looks ashamed in front of his mother.

Let's face it; many Christians do not know how to overcome a recurrent sin. They will be surprised by the answer below.

Just as without faith, it is impossible to please God, without faith, it will be impossible for Christians to triumph over a sin that disturbs them. In fact, no earthly medicament can really work. People of the world have created "anonymous" groups where those with the same addiction meet to share personal experiences. It is by faith that the Christian triumphs over sin, faith being defined as *the substance of things hoped for, the evidence of things not seen* **(Hebrews 11:1)**.

Jesus bore all the sins of Christians on the cross of Golgotha, as well as their addictions. Why do Christians still have to suffer the effects of it? Certainly, sin is a living reality, whether rude or minor. However, the Christian must believe that he has been delivered by the Lord who does not lie – even if presently the Christian is suffering of sin and ashamed of it. Then he will see the glory of God by discovering that sin has disappeared.

The problem for Christians is that they no longer want to see the slightest sin affect their bodies. They are right but faith remains faith. Without faith, they can neither please God nor obtain anything. The Lord wants faith rather than meetings for 'anonymous' or other weird prescriptions – like Yoga. God wants faith in what Jesus accomplished on the cross. Please watch out; by these, we do not discourage people to attain 'anonymous' meetings because after all, faith is a private commitment. Everyone does as he pleases.

The other problem is the ignorance of Christians about the experiences of other Christians in the world. All Christians around the world at one time had to face recalcitrant sins. Some had relief immediately. Others waited, relying on faith.

It is time to remember that heroes of the Bible also faced sins and uncomfortable dramas. Not only those of the Old Testament like Moses at Meriba, David about the General

Uriah he sent to death after committing adultery with his wife. Apostle Paul also faced many sins. He declares for example, "***What I hate, that I do (...) Now it is no more I that do it, but sin that dwells in me***" (**Romans 7:15, 17**). By saying ***what I hate, that I do***, Paul implicitly acknowledged that he did sin despite efforts not to do it. At the end of this sad statement about the irreparably sinful human condition, Paul made an important discovery: "*There is therefore now **no condemnation to those who are in Christ Jesus, who walk not according to the flesh but according to the Spirit**. But the law of the Spirit of life in Christ Jesus has made me free from the law of sin and death*" (**Romans 8:1-2**). Basically, it is by walking by the Spirit – or by faith – that the Christian will triumph over sin.

From the statement above, one triumphs over sin, **firstly** knowing that, upon the occurrence of sin, the Lord Jesus will not condemn him as during the Old Testament's time. The Christian is forgiven when he confesses his sins. Apostle Paul did not say: *Eureka! I do not sin anymore!* He said rather: *There is therefore now no condemnation...* Apparently, it is not the disappearance of sin that interests Apostle Paul here, but the fact that the sinner is no longer condemned as during the Old Testament's time.

Secondly, as a result of the above observation, sin is swept by walking by the Spirit. To walk by the Spirit is to walk by faith. To walk by faith is to APPLY (KEEP) the commandments of Jesus Christ as expressed during His three-year earthly pilgrimage, and as resumed in great detail by His servants the Apostles.

In concrete terms, do you deal with a recalcitrant sin that keeps coming back? First, relax knowing that you are not under a condemnation sentence. Be careful, sin is bad. It is your sin that is hated by the Lord, not you. Your sin is doomed, not you. It is as if the devil made your body sin to get you away of Christianity. He distills you with the words "*You are not holy and will never be. Look at that mess you are in. You are a condemned sinner, recidivist, unrepentant. Look at yourself; does a saint sin like that? You are not holy. You deceive yourself by thinking that you are holy ...*" Relax and do NOT FEEL GUILTY because your condemnation has already fallen on Jesus at the cross of Golgotha. And as Jesus died, the criminal case against Him – the scapegoat – is extinguished. The sin you get trapped in is certainly odious, but without any jail constraint. The Lord does not condemn you because He has already dealt with your condemnation at Golgotha. That is to say, rejoice that the door of heaven is not closed for you.

Does this mean that the Lord is asking you to rejoice in the sin knowing that you will not be condemned? No, absolutely no. Remember what Jesus said to the adulteress: *Go and sin no more*. Jesus doesn't like sin. He doesn't like to see the Christian sinning. But in pursuing an unrelenting sanctification, consisting in obeying the commandments of the Lord, sin's episode will gradually fade away. Jesus will have taken His revenge on sin and on the devil: *O death, where is your sting?* (**1 Corinthians 15:55**) The Bible further states:

> **«*That he suffering in the flesh has been made to rest from sin*» (1 Peter 4:1).**

> **«*And this is the victory that overcomes the world, our faith*» (1 John 5:4).**

These two verses show that the victory over sin is obtained by faith, and not by programs the world is used to – "anonymous". And it is by following a relentless sanctification that the body will see the sins stop to martyrize him. Amen.

On the spot, must we passively wait for deliverance? Like the young child, ashamed in front of his mother after he pissed on, the Christian is ashamed in front of his God when he is caught in the entrails of sin. And as the young child, growing up, sees these sores disappear one by one – he stops pissing on – the Christian, by dint of sanctification, triumphs over sin. The Christian must therefore feel ashamed and secretly cry to God. This is what David did after his crime over General Uriah, his servant, was revealed. God will hear the cries of the Christian and will act accordingly. However, He will do it in His time and not according to the wishes of the Christian whom He cherishes yet. Patience is therefore essential in the process of triumphing over any sin. The Christian can rightly know that His God loves him despite the sin. God does not love sin, but He loves His Christian and cherishes Him. Amen.

Love, the most formidable weapon to triumph in Jesus Christ

> «*This is My commandment, that **you love one another** as I have loved you*» **John 15:12**.

> «*Faith, hope, love, these three remain; but the greatest of these is love*» (**1 Corinthians 13:13**).

> «*And above all things have fervent love to yourselves, for **love will cover a multitude of sins***» (**1 Peter 4:8**).

In reading that *love is greater than faith and hope* (**1 Corinthians 13:13**), I admit that I was surprised by the way the Apostle made his words so clear. Here, Paul does not doubt, nor introduces an element of uncertainty. It is clear as if there is nothing to object. And that's where my curiosity got excited. There are many Bible verses of the same type, but few people pay attention as if they were to be content with the minimum in the Word of God. Imagine a cook who offers his best meal and, in return, only a few sips are swallowed by the guests. Will he be happy? Many Christians irritate God by limiting their reading to the bare minimum as if they were to get rid of His Word and move on. What else is it? Jesus has repeatedly compared the Word of God to a food. He recalled that *man shall not live by bread alone, but by every word that proceeds out of the mouth of God* (**Matthew 4:4**). The Word of God is therefore a fortifying food, and whoever underestimates it, will miss the most important nutrients of life. In contrast, the usual bread provides a passing pleasure before being digested and rejected.

It must be admitted that love is more important than faith and hope, or even the most important thing. Yet of faith it is said that it is with it that the Christian *will quench all the fiery darts of the wicked* (**Ephesians 6:16**). Is it his formidable efficiency towards the enemy that makes faith so popular among Christians and more popular than love? It can be said so because what kind of relationship would exist between God and men if the devil had not made the habit of upsetting the earth? Faith is very popular among Christians because, let's say it, they need it to counter Satan.

But if the Bible says that love is more important than faith, there is a reason we should find out.

The fact is that faith – like hope – is primarily a matter of posture before being an action to be performed. For example, Abraham was content to believe, without any notable action, and his faith awarded him all the credit of God's justice. The Bible insists that any action without faith cannot please God. We don't claim that faith means zero action, let alone having faith without the evidence of faith. Above all, we want to say that, unlike faith, love is primarily a matter of action. Love-posture is not always love. To say that one loves is not more significant than to affirm the opposite. If you tell someone that you love him, he will answer *"thank you"* no more, with a friendly smile. If rather you tell him that you hate him, he will go away with a shrug of spite. Verbal love does not make so much impression. But the acts of love speak more than anything. Everywhere, the Word of God insists on action as evidence of faith. So love-action is evidence that faith is present. It is because love confirms faith that the Apostle has certainly placed love above faith and hope. An act of love does not lie. While the declaration of love alone can conceal a deep hatred.

The Bible confirms these above words:

> *«If anyone says, I love God, and hates his brother, he is a liar. For **if he does not love his brother whom he has seen, how can he love God whom he has not seen?**» (**1 John 4:20**)*

> *«Whoever has this world's goods and sees his brother having need, and shuts up his bowels from him, **how does the***

***love of God dwell in him?*»** **(1 John 3:17)**

«*And though I have prophecies, and understand all mysteries and all knowledge; and though I have all faith, so as to move mountains, **and do not have love, I am nothing***» **(1 Corinthians 13:2)**.

Putting the Word of God in practice after reading it is evidence that love is active. The Lord said not to respond to blows, but *to turn your cheek,* not to take revenge, but to leave it to Him. Many think that they can change the gospel by distorting the verses' meaning or avoiding to put it in practice. Far from me to say that it's easy to take shots without answering. But it is better to obey the Lord despite the difficulty of it. Many Christians confessed that they did not understand why they had let go an offense – they usually fought back – as if an invisible force had restrained them. This is evidence that the Lord lives in that Christian to do the will of His Father who is in heaven. It is enough for the Christian to trust Him and he will see himself carrying out the commandments of God, which are difficult to apply on a human scale.

The path of victory remains that of faith, while love is the visible evidence that confirms that one has faith. Without love, faith is tasteless, vain and empty. The Lord warns us against it. But *Love has patience, is kind; love is not envious, is not vain, is not puffed up; does not behave indecently, does not seek his own, is not easily provoked, thinks no evil. Love does not rejoice in unrighteousness, but rejoices in the truth* (**1 Corinthians 13:4-8**).

He who obeys the commandments of the Lord, such as *turning his cheek, giving up his second tunic, or walking another mile*, testifies that he is humble. And *humility precedes glory*. On the other hand, whoever does not obey, displays his arrogance. But *arrogance precedes disaster*.

In exhorting us to love one another, Jesus knew what love would cost us, because to love is to turn your cheek, give up your second tunic, and make an extra mile.

The Christian triumphs over loneliness

> *«And I will pray the Father, and He shall give you another Comforter,* **so that He may be with you forever,** *the Spirit of truth, whom the world cannot receive because it does not see Him nor know Him. But you know Him,* **for He dwells with you and shall be in you. I will not leave you orphans. I will come to you»** **John 14:16-18.**

> *«Do you not know that* **your body is a temple of the Holy Spirit in you, whom you have of God?** *And you are not your own»* **1 Corinthians 6:19.**

Loneliness – being alone – is an aspect of life that is dreaded. Finding yourself alone is a feeling of unsustainable distress. The one who is alone is afraid of a threat, real or imagined, that could put his life in danger. Who will help me in case of serious danger? Is the question that regularly concerns the lonely.

But the Christian must rest reassured: he does not have to fear loneliness because he is no longer alone and will never be alone again. This is sustained by Jesus Christ's word:

> «*And, behold, **I am with you all the days until the end of the world**»* (**Matthew 28:20**).

How does one feel the presence of God?

Many Christians always asked themselves this question, and they are right because God is their Father. It is quite normal for Christians to care about the Father they love and cherish. I have also asked myself this question many times, especially at the beginning of my Christian faith. Unlike humans who appreciate the presence of loved ones they can see, Christians' difficulty in feeling the presence of the invisible God is source of frustration.

However everything begins with faith because *without faith, it is impossible to please God*. Faith is the subject of many definitions, all similar, with different words. Faith is believing that what the Scripture says is real – though still invisible – and then we can touch its reality with fingers when it becomes visible. We insist on the fact that **faith must relate to what Scripture says and not to what human tradition say**. 'Think positive' consists of staring a good intention at a goal for it to come true. This is neither the definition nor the understanding that Scripture gives of faith. Apostle John declares:

> «*If we ask anything **according to His will, He hears us**. And if we know that He hears us, whatever we ask, we know that we have the petitions that we desired of Him*» (**1 John 5:14-15**).

It is well stipulated **according to the will of God**. It is not a question of multiplying positive thoughts and crying out: *I have already prayed!* The Bible is clear. **Faith refers to what Scripture says, not to what we think for ourselves**.

Thus because Jesus says *He is with the Christian all the days until the end of the world,* the Christian must accept this as true, even if none of his five senses feel this reality. Jesus having said it, then it is true. You do not have to rely on your senses to make this statement credible. When the Scripture says: *true*, faith replies: *true*. There is nothing to add.

Let us not forget the second part of the definition of faith according to the Bible: "*Faith is (1) the substance of things hoped for, (2) **the evidence of things not seen**"* (**Hebrews 11:1**). The *substance of things hoped for* defines what has been said above. The *evidence of things not seen* refers to the promise of God to give form to what is expected by faith. He who has faith, as defined above, will see with his own eyes what he expects. It is the apparition of what was hidden – promised – that makes the evidence. Once we see with our own eyes what we have hoped for, then God completes the evidence. This is why Scripture ends the definition of faith by '*the evidence of things not seen*'.

When the Christian accepts that Jesus walks every day near him, he gradually discovers that SOMEONE is ALWAYS standing inside him and beside him. This person is none other than JESUS CHRIST in the form of the Holy Spirit promised by Him. More importantly whenever the Christian faces an earthly crisis, the Holy Spirit living within him raises thoughts of appeasement and relaxation. Just saying to him: *Do not worry, I saw it coming. There is nothing to be alarmed. I control the situation. Cool down.* Gradually, quietness will settle in the heart of the Christian despite the storm around. Such is the assurance of Christians, sometimes to the dismay of pagans who usually take this posture for arrogance or inconsistency. But they are pagans. Christians do not have to worry about it.

The presence of God and the posture of Mary Madeleine

«As they went, it happened that Jesus entered into a certain village. And a certain woman named Martha received Him into her house. And she had a sister called Mary, who also **sat at Jesus' feet** *and heard His word. But Martha was distracted with much serving. And she came to Him and said, Lord, do You not care that my sister has left me to serve alone? Therefore tell her to help me. And Jesus answered and said to her, Martha, Martha, you are anxious and troubled about many things. But one thing is needful, and Mary has chosen that good part, which shall not be taken away from her»* **(Luke 10:38-42***)*.

Martha who was worried about the precious guests was wrong about Mary's behavior, yet caught in the act of laziness. How can one appreciate a blameworthy immobility to the detriment of the eagerness to serve? If Martha had not served the guests, who would have cared? We can begin by analyzing the reaction of the Lord, favorable to Mary: *Martha, you are anxious and troubled about many things. But one thing is needful, and Mary has chosen that good part...* Can a lazy girl be appreciated at the expense of an active worker?

The peculiarity of this scene lies in the fact that the Lord admonished Martha, who in the eyes of many humans, deserved praise. Instead the Lord appreciated the inactive Mary who stood close to Him.

The attitude of the Lord is very significant because He admonished a virtuous person from a human perspective. In fact Martha makes herself available and gives it all to others. Isn't it honorable? But the Lord has a different opinion here: He gives wrong to Martha and right to Mary. Here, Mary stares at the Lord without being distracted by things that are apparently useful, but futile in their purpose. Are we often too busy to the point of not focusing on the Lord? As the Lord said, Mary had found the good part, hence the question: what was it? This is the place for truly question the foundations of Christian's faith because the risks of being wrong remain. What does the Lord really expect from the Christian? To stir for a good cause or to seek Him? According to the above Bible verses, Martha was busy to serve the guests, while Mary seated inactive at the Lord's feet. It did not matter to Mary that the guests were present and numerous, only the presence of the Lord counted. Her joy was complete in a posture of total contemplation of the Lord.

Mary was happy to be in the presence of the Lord. Between Mary Madeleine and Jesus Christ, the communion was so strong that the guests' concern took second place.

Jesus' attitude towards Martha did not consist in saying that Martha had been doing bad in serving the guests. Jesus said that Mary chose the best part. If Martha had sinned, Jesus would have admonished her. Instead Jesus let us know that, dislike Martha, He rather preferred the posture of Mary.

The attitude of Mary, insensitive to the guests, but focused on the Lord, was appreciated by God.

We conclude by talking about the benefits of God's presence. Mary was in the presence of the Lord God. God being the true life, His presence is a source of life and strength that boosts everything. Remember Moses who spent forty days and forty nights without drinking or eating. It was not a fast, contrary to what I've read in some books. Before going to meet God on the Sinai Mountain, Moses had already prescribed three days of fasting to the Israelites, consisting of not eating delicacies and not having sexual intercourse. These three days were the real fast, while the forty days spent in the presence of God kept Moses from famine and thirst. The presence of God was enough. Let us also remember how the face of Moses shone with brilliance because of his continual staring at the ark of the testimony where God revealed Himself to him. It is to say how the presence of God is exalting and strengthening.

Loneliness, a strength for the Christian

The Bible relates several cases of the servants of God facing loneliness. From what we remember, loneliness was a force, not a moment of anguish, because loneliness is an opportunity to talk to God away from the spotlight of the world. The Christian transforms his moments of loneliness into special occasions of talking with God on all matters that count, without taboos.

Honestly, the Lord wishes to have private moments with His beloved Christian, to talk to him on all matters of life. But the Christian often goes distracted, without regard to the Lord who stands yet close to him. The Lord therefore takes advantage of moments of loneliness to invite Himself in the meditation of this Christian. Jesus loves talking without taboos. Thus, when the Christian thinks to be alone, he is not so because the Lord stands right near him ready for a talk. Such is the strength of the Christian. He is not alone and will never be alone. The Lord is his and he is happy with it.

The Christian's light triumphs over darkness

We will talk about two forms of darkness. The one considered as the den of the devil and obscure practices, and the other defined as the absence of light.

The Christian triumphs over the devil's darkness

Jesus told His disciples:

> *«Behold, I give to you **authority to tread** on serpents and scorpions, and **over all the authority of the enemy**. And nothing shall by any means hurt you»* (**Luke 10:19**).

By these words, there is no doubt that the Christian is now above the forces of darkness since Jesus gave him ***authority to tread*** *on serpents and scorpions, and **over all the authority of the enemy***. It is very clear: the Christian is above the power of the enemy, Satan.

Apostle John confirms it by saying:

> *«You are of God, little children, and you have overcome them, because **He who is in you is greater than he who is in the world»** (**1 John 4:4**).*

The devil is the one literally designated as *he who is in the world*, while the Holy Spirit is *He who is in the Christian,* since Jesus Himself said that the Holy Spirit, the Comforter, would be ***in the Christian and with him*** when He comes – this is effective since Pentecost.

That being said, the attitude and posture of the Christian should comply accordingly. Many people around the world have been in touch with the forces of darkness: witchcraft, magic, spells, vampirism, astral projection, forbidden sexual intercourse, Satanism, necrophagy, sodomy, zoophilia, astrology, voodoo, ritual sacrifice, transubstantiation, etc. The Lord warns the Christian to end any relationship with the world of darkness by abstaining from these practices. Moses already warned the Israelites newly freed from Egyptian slavery, a country they had been living in for four hundred years, accustomed to local beliefs and practices.

> *«There shall not be found among you anyone who makes his son or his daughter to pass through the fire, or **that uses divination, an observer of clouds, or a fortune-teller, or a witch, or a***

> ***charmer, or a consulter with familiar spirits, or a wizard, or one who calls to the dead.*** *For all that do these things are an abomination to Jehovah. (...)* ***You shall be perfect with Jehovah your God.*** *For these nations whom you shall possess listened to observers of clouds and to diviners.* ***But as for you, Jehovah your God has not allowed you to do so»*** **(Deuteronomy 18:10-14).**

God recognizes that by being separated from Him since the tragedy of Eden Garden, man had no choice but to rely on the army of heaven to read and know the future. But to His Christians, God no longer allows it. His people should part way with it. By the call to cast these practices, God separates the Christian from any contact with the occult world, that of darkness in particular.

Christians must take the utmost care to get away from these practices. Any violation of this instruction will expose them to worse damages, generally irreversible. Many can testify it with tears and bitterness. By staying away from these practices, with God alone as a protective shield, without any other form of support (potion or elixir of any kind), the Christian will definitely be safe from these inconveniences. We know that the devil will not remain inactive. He will multiply provocations, just to remind the Christian that he is still connected to the kingdom of darkness that he claims to have quit. No matter the provocation (paralysis during sleep, wet dreams, occult rashes, etc.), the Christian must not panic. It is enough for him to stand up to these provocations and pronounce the judgment of God against them like: "*Satan, demons, human spirits in the service of Satan: I condemn your actions and you are to move away from my body because God delivered me from the power of darkness and carried me into the kingdom of His beloved Son. There is nothing left between you and me. My body now belongs to Christ. Get out in the name of Jesus Christ, the King of kings!*"

The devil knows the Word of God well since he had already recalled it with great details during the *temptation of Christ*. He also knows the Christian's rights. With this pray, the devil has no choice but to leave. The Christian can go back to sleep peacefully, without being afraid of consequences of the attack he has just suffered. We specify that during these attacks, the Christian may feel embarrassed to the satisfaction of the enemy whose aim is to create doubt in his faith. But the Christian must stand firm and not fall into the trap set by the devil. The Bible says:

> «*Resist the devil, and he will flee from you*» (**James 4:7**).

> «*Your adversary the devil walks about like a roaring lion, seeking someone he may devour;* **whom firmly resist in the faith**, *knowing that the same afflictions*

in the world are being completed in your brotherhood» (**1 Peter 5:8-9**).

Do not get fooled by appearances. The devil is a champion in the art of pretense and illusions. Trust only the Word of God and he will flee from you. Rashes of dubious origin and any other skin manifestation will disappear as if they had never happened.

Don't be afraid. It is clear that abandoning practices that have "shielded" you for many years seems difficult to grasp. This is what Satan relies on to keep you under control for a long time. Break! Break! It's your lifeline. Keeping a link, however small, is a big mistake.

The Christian triumphs over darkness as lack of light

Jesus told His disciples:

«You are the light of the world» (**Matthew 5:14**).

Let's linger a little on the relationship between light and darkness. Science says that *darkness is the absence of light*, a way of saying that when light appears, darkness disappears. There is no fight because light is reflected in clarity, while darkness is the absence of light. Absence has no substance.

When light appears, darkness disappears because, without form or substance, darkness cannot oppose resistance.

By saying that the Christian is the light of the world, the Lord implies that it is for the Christian to appear somewhere for the darkness to vanish. More importantly, the darkness pulls the man down: impure thoughts, theft, crime, despondency, distress, resignation, degeneration ... death. While the light pulls him up where God sits: thoughts and wisdom from above, love, encouragement, hope ... life.

The Christian must become aware of his status and the grace that is given him to be the temple of the Holy Spirit. As such, he is more valuable than the temple of Moses, so dreaded in the time of Old Testament. So dreaded that anyone who was considered impure, daring to approach it, was put to death. The Holy Spirit had never come down on the temple of Moses. Apostle Paul says of this time that it was the angels' worship, hence the need for Moses as mediator (**Galatians 3:19**) unlike Jesus who did not need a mediator (V20) to dispatch His gospel. Jesus is the High Priest for eternity according to Melchizedek's priesthood.

Dear Christian, if you are sons of light, stay in the light and do not come down. Keep your thoughts up to the heavens of God. Avoid going down to the darkness that is there.

Table of Contents

www.ingramcontent.com/pod-product-compliance
Lightning Source LLC
Chambersburg PA
CBHW071512150726
48000CB00002B/553